Feel Good Kitchen

FEEL GOOD KITCHEN
Amy Lanza

First published in the UK and USA in 2025 by
Nourish, an imprint of Watkins Media Limited
Unit 11, Shepperton House, 83–93 Shepperton Road,
London N1 3DF

enquiries@nourishbooks.com

Publisher: Fiona Robertson
Commissioning Editor: Lucy Carroll
Editorial Manager: Daniel Culver
Copyeditor: Sophie Elletson
Head of Design: Karen Smith
Design Concept: Francesca Corsini
Layout: Abi Hartshorne/Karen Smith
Production: Uzma Taj
Commissioned photography: Amy Lanza
Nutritionist: Eli Brecher

A CIP record for this book is available from
the British Library

ISBN: 978-1-84899-439-3 (Hardback)
ISBN: 978-1-84899-420-1 (eBook)

10 9 8 7 6 5 4 3 2 1

Typeset in Sofia Pro & Gazpacho

Printed in China

Publisher's note
While every care has been taken in compiling the
recipes for this book, Watkins Media Limited, or any
other persons who have been involved in working
on this publication, cannot accept responsibility for
any errors or omissions, inadvertent or not, that may
be found in the recipes or text, nor for any problems
that may arise as a result of preparing one of these
recipes. If you are pregnant or breastfeeding or
have any special dietary requirements or medical
conditions, it is advisable to consult a medical
professional before following any of the recipes
contained in this book.

Notes on the recipes
Unless otherwise stated:
Use medium fruit and vegetables
Use fresh herbs, spices and chillies
Do not mix metric, imperial and
US cup measurements:
1 tsp = 5ml
1 tbsp = 15ml
1 cup = 240ml

nourishbooks.com

Feel Good Kitchen

80 PLANT-BASED RECIPES TO BOOST YOUR MOOD AND NOURISH YOUR BRAIN

Amy Lanza

FOUNDER OF NOURISHING AMY

NOURISH

EAT WELL, LIVE WELL

contents

009 Introduction

PART 1

healthy brain

022 Breakfast

046 Lunch

068 Dinner

090 Snacks & Desserts

PART 2

happy mind

112 Breakfast

138 Lunch

160 Dinner

182 Snacks & Desserts

206 About the author

207 Acknowledgments

208 Index

INTRODUCTION

Welcome to Feel Good Kitchen: 80 Plant-based Recipes to Boost your Mood and Nourish your Brain! I am so honoured you are holding this in your hands. This new cookbook has been created as a toolkit to help you feel your best every day. Through vibrant plant-based recipes, mindful meals and focusing on healthful ingredients, I aim to showcase how delicious, exciting and nourishing food can be –and how good it can make you feel.

Plants are powerful and they allow us to nourish our bodies in a way that feels right for us; whether you are looking for a delicious high-protein dinner, a brain-boosting breakfast or a nostalgic and mood-boosting dessert, this cookbook celebrates all plant-based foods, so you can create more of what you love.

From breakfast and brunch to lunch, dinner and dessert, there is something for everyone in this cookbook. This book is designed for you to come back to time and time again, trying out one or two recipes a week or to fully embrace a plant-based lifestyle and eat dishes from this collection of recipes all week long.

Enjoy these recipes as part of a balanced lifestyle that includes good-quality sleep, drinking enough water, exercising regularly, practising mindful breathing and doing things just for you! Self-care is one of the best things we can prioritize to really help elevate the kitchen magic within this cookbook.

I hope you'll find exactly what you're looking for in this book (and then read on to try out more), and remember that balance really is the key to overall health and wellbeing.

How to Use Feel Good Kitchen

This collection of delicious recipes is divided into two sections: Healthy Brain and Happy Mind. Together, they encompass a 360-degree approach to food, eating and sharing in the enjoyment of mealtimes. Only when we focus on the whole picture can we truly nourish our bodies and minds. Throughout each section, you'll discover much-loved favourites with a wholesome vegan spin, as well as exciting flavoursome creations to tempt all taste buds: this is food for all day, every day. Throughout the book, I have highlighted key ingredients and nutrients that will inform your decisions on which recipes you choose. A few running themes throughout Feel Good Kitchen include to listen to your body, to eat a wide variety of colours and food groups and to understand your food to ultimately lead to feel-good food freedom.

Healthy Brain

Eating for your brain is one of the best things we can do for overall longevity and great long-term health. The food we eat is the fuel on which our brain runs, so nourishing it with high-quality and nutrient-dense foods enables us to feel our best. While there are many brain-boosting foods, this chapter will focus on a few key wholefood staples (you probably know them already as they are everyday ingredients) that are seen to increase brain function, improve memory and protect it from stress.

Throughout this chapter, you'll see ingredients crop up time and time again, most of which contain high levels of antioxidants, B vitamins, healthy fats and omega-3 fatty acids. These are easy to incorporate into your everyday, with brain-boosting breakfasts, vibrant lunches, delicious dinners, snacks and desserts to keep you feeling sharp. These are also nutritionally balanced, so you can eat from this chapter all day long and know that your brain will thank you later.

Key ingredients to include:

Avocados are loaded with healthy unsaturated fats that reduce blood pressure and prevent cognitive decline. They are great for the brain and monounsaturated fats also promote healthy blood flow.

Tea and coffee contain caffeine, which is a natural brain booster. They are a great source of polyphenols which have several benefits such as lowering blood pressure, improving brain health and cognitions and being a source of antioxidants to promote better brain health as you age. But be warned: too much of a good thing will leave you feeling jittery and disrupt your sleep cycle.

Berries and oranges are high in antioxidants which can benefit learning and memory by increasing the brain's plasticity, improving connections between brain cells and fighting free radicals. They are high in vitamin C which may protect brain cells from age-related damage.

Dark/bittersweet chocolate is amazing to include in your diet, as it is a powerhouse of antioxidants and natural stimulants like caffeine. It is also shown to improve memory and mood, while the flavonoids within dark chocolate aid learning and memory formation. Remember to choose dairy-free dark, milk and white chocolate (I mainly use dark chocolate in my recipes).

Nuts and seeds (in particular chia seeds and flaxseed) contain high levels of omega-3 fatty acids (good healthy fats) and antioxidants, making them a major brain food. It is thought that regular consumption of these can reduce the risk of age-related memory loss, and while all nuts and seeds have specific benefits, walnuts make the best brain food as they have the highest levels of antioxidants (they are also shaped like the brain, so you can see why!).

Dark leafy vegetables (like kale, broccoli and spinach) are an excellent source of fibre, folate and carotenoids. These vegetables also contain vitamins C and K and B vitamins as well as being a source of iron and calcium. Plus, they are known for their antioxidant properties.

Happy Mind

Eating is one of life's greatest joys and whether you are cooking for one or two or feeding a crowd, being present with your food choices and eating mindfully only heightens the experience. Food can play a huge factor in our mental health and can also create specific feelings within us: there are foods which leave us feeling nostalgic and happy, meals which we can feast our eyes upon, and ones which shroud us in a cosy cocoon. In this way, your food choices will be personal to you, so remember to eat what makes you feel your best. Note that there is a lot of crossover with the brain section, as our brain is closely linked with our mood.

While there are many ingredients within this chapter, one group which I love to focus on is fermented foods. Evolving scientific research on gut health continues to support a strong link between gut health and overall health with long- and short-term impacts on our brain function. Benefits may include reducing stress, improving digestion and enhancing mental health via the gut-brain axis. This is a two-way communication link and explains why stress may cause digestive problems and those with IBS may experience feelings of anxiety. The gut and brain are chemically connected via neurotransmitters such as serotonin, aka the happy hormone (of which 90% is produced in the gut!). So, you really should learn to trust your "gut feeling". Foods which feed our gut are known as probiotic foods and contain live microorganisms that maintain the good microflora in our gut (think of it like a garden and the more diverse our diets are, the more vibrant our gardens can be, allowing them to flourish). Prebiotics, on the other hand, are dietary fibre that feed our gut microbes, allowing them to produce nutrients in the gut. A diet rich in both pre- and probiotics are important for our overall wellbeing.

Key ingredients to focus on:

Fermented foods such as kimchi, sauerkraut, tofu, miso and live dairy-free yogurt contain probiotic bacteria to support the gut-brain axis. Their ability to boost good gut bacteria has been linked in studies to help combat depression.

Bananas are high in vitamin B6, which helps synthesize the feel-good neurotransmitters like dopamine and serotonin (great for good mood) and they are a natural sugar. This makes them great for sweetening recipes without a blood sugar spike, while they also contain prebiotics, which help to feed healthy bacteria in the gut.

Oats are an amazing whole grain and are a great source of fibre, which allows for the gradual release of sugar in the bloodstream to keep energy levels stable (important for controlling mood swings and preventing us feeling "hangry").

Brazil nuts are particularly high in selenium, which may help reduce inflammation, support brain function and improve thyroid function and heart health. Other nuts and seeds (such as almonds, cashews and peanuts and pumpkin, sesame and sunflower seeds) contain tryptophan, an amino acid responsible for producing mood-boosting serotonin.

Eating the rainbow has never been more important. Not only do rainbow meals look pleasing to the eye, but different-coloured fruits and vegetables contain different minerals and vitamins. Leafy greens contain magnesium to boost your mood, while avocado helps the stress response thanks to the phytochemicals within the fruit. Also, berries contain a group of flavonoids called anthocyanins which have shown to help reduce feelings of depression.

Foods high in polyphenols (such as tea and coffee mentioned before, as well as dark/bittersweet chocolate, fruits and vegetables, more generally) have a prebiotic effect in the body, meaning they feed the beneficial probiotics in the gut.

Shopping List

Here is a guide to some of my favourite ingredients to keep in your kitchen so that you can make the recipes in this book.

Fresh Produce

Different-coloured fruits and vegetables contain a variety of vitamins and minerals, so eating the rainbow really is the best thing you can do for your body. Eating seasonally is also really important in terms of sustainability, getting the optimum nutrition from your foods and for price, too, so always try to opt for seasonal specialities, when you can. I use fresh herbs a lot in my recipes as they add flavour and colour to many dishes and also provide a lovely finishing touch. Fresh herbs are also a good source of vitamins and minerals.

Fruits I eat regularly:

Berries (fresh and/or frozen are great) like blueberries, raspberries, strawberries and blackberries

Apples and pears

Stoned fruits like plums, peaches, cherries and apricots

Bananas (easy as a snack, for baking with and for making smoothies)

Avocados

Tomatoes

Lemons and limes

Oranges, satsumas or other peelable citrus fruit

Vegetables I eat regularly:

Dark leafy greens like kale, cavolo nero and spinach

Salad greens e.g. rocket/ arugula, watercress, lettuce

Salad vegetables like cucumber and radishes

Carrots

Cabbage and spring/ collard greens

Potatoes and sweet potatoes

Cruciferous produce like broccoli, Brussels sprouts and cauliflower

Aubergines/eggplants

Mushrooms

Onions (white, red and spring onions/scallions)

Garlic

Root ginger

Fresh chillies (you can use them with or without

the seeds, depending on your spice tolerance and preference). I usually use the red ones, and remember that each chilli is different so check the spiciness each time.

Fresh herbs I use regularly:

Parsley

Coriander/cilantro

Mint

Basil

Chives

Freezer Items

I mainly use the freezer to keep leftover meals and bakes, but I always have stock of the following:

Edamame beans

Frozen peas like petit pois

Frozen courgettes/zucchini and bananas that I have previously sliced

Bread (e.g. sourdough, rye or homemade), so that it lasts longer

Frozen berries (either a mixed bag or individual ones for smoothies and porridge toppings)

Dairy-free Essentials

There are a few plant-based alternatives to dairy that are very useful to keep in the refrigerator and/or store cupboard:

Dairy-free, plant-based milks. Always look for ones with minimal ingredients, without additives, thickeners or gums where possible, to be as natural as possible. My favourites include oat, almond, soya and coconut milk. You can buy these fresh to keep in the refrigerator, or long-life cartons, too. If using dairy-free milks in savoury recipes, ensure they are unsweetened.

Thick coconut yogurt. I use the thick and creamy type of yogurt with minimal ingredients which mimics Greek-style yogurt in texture and is great for sweet and savoury dishes (ensure it's unsweetened for savoury recipes, but a vanilla flavour is great for baking). My go-to brand is Cocos Organic.

Vegan cream cheese. There are a few in the shops and these are great for frostings, or you can easily make your own following my recipe on page 198.

Vegan butter doesn't feature heavily in this book, but there are some good block-style or spreadable dairy-free butters in supermarkets

Ice creams, custards and creams are all optional extras for recipes – there are some lovely dairy-free versions in the dairy or free-from aisles and they can be replaced like-for-like for dairy items.

Store Cupboard Staples

Make the most of your kitchen cupboards, so you can whip up delicious recipes in no time at all. I like to have a selection of:

Canned tomatoes (also including tomato passata/sieved tomatoes and tomato purée/paste).

Canned or jarred beans like chickpeas/garbanzo beans, butter/lima beans, cannellini beans, black beans, red kidney beans and cooked lentils.

Canned sweetcorn kernels

Canned coconut milk in light and full-fat versions (also available in cartons). Where a recipe calls for full-fat coconut milk, you have to use this as there is more cream, which is essential for the recipe. But in other places where you can choose, the full-fat version will be creamier overall.

Coconut oil, olive oil (both light, regular and extra virgin), avocado oil and nut/seed oils. These are all useful to have in your cupboard and they have their own benefits and uses. You can mostly swap between them, but it's best to follow the recipe suggestion. I also have an olive oil spray which is easy to use, but not essential.

Tamari soy sauce (this is gluten-free, regular soy sauce is not)

Hot chilli sauce like sriracha

Lemon and/or lime juice jars (check they are 100% juice)

Apple cider vinegar is great to have on hand for making homemade buttermilk and for salad dressings

Vanilla extract is key for baking (not to be confused with vanilla essence which is synthetic and inferior in flavour, so always choose vanilla extract)

Raw cacao powder and unsweetened cocoa powder are both used throughout the book. As a general rule, I use raw cacao powder for raw recipes, like smoothies and frostings, but I'll use unsweetened cocoa powder for baking, as it is more acidic and creates a better texture and rise in cakes. Always look for 100% unsweetened cacao and cocoa powders.

Apple sauce is a really useful ingredient and you can find it in most supermarkets or health food shops. This is 100% unsweetened apple sauce and not to be confused with the savoury apple sauce used for dinners. It usually comes in jars and is stored at room temperature until opened.

Salt and pepper are both essential for adding flavour and seasoning to your food. I use a flaky and regular sea salt (my favourites are Maldon or Cornish Sea Salt) and I have whole black peppercorns which I grind in a pepper mill and use throughout the book. I also love grinding pink and black peppercorns together, if you have those.

Grains and Pulses

There are so many whole grains to choose from, and as diversity is key, where you see one whole grain option, feel free to swap it with another of your choice. I like:

Quinoa (tricolour or white)

Rice (particularly short-grain brown rice and sticky rice) and orzo

Noodles (buckwheat, soba or rice noodles are gluten-free)

Pasta (opt for whole grain where you can, and choose gluten-free where needed) in a variety of shapes. Note that fresh pasta often contains egg, so watch out if buying it fresh.

Buckwheat (actually a pseudo-grain)

Couscous (this is not naturally gluten-free)

Freekeh (also not gluten-free)

Bulgur wheat (this does contain gluten)

Spelt (this also contains gluten)

Wholegrain tortilla wraps, pitta breads and naan breads (choose gluten-free where needed)

Fermented Foods

These are so important for overall health, as well as our gut. A few of my favourites include:

Kimchi and sauerkraut (check they are vegan as some contain fish)

Tofu: extra-firm and silken are both used throughout the book. Extra-firm tofu is perfect for cubing, frying, grating and scrambling, whereas silken tofu is great for high-protein sauces and cheesecakes!

Miso paste (I use white and brown rice miso pastes the most often)

Nuts and Seeds

These feature heavily throughout the book as they are a great source of healthy fatty acids and are real mood and brain boosters. Here is a selection of nuts and seeds I like to have at home:

Walnuts

Brazil nuts

Almonds

Cashews

Hazelnuts

Pecans

Pistachios

Sunflower seeds

Pumpkin seeds

Mixed seeds (a selection bag)

Chia seeds

Ground and whole flaxseed

Hulled hemp seeds

Sesame seeds (white and/ or black)

Coconut (not technically a nut or seed but I like to have desiccated/dried shredded and flaked coconut)

As for **Nut and seed butters**, always look for the ones that are 100% nut/seed or with some salt as the only other ingredient. Where a recipe uses nut butter, you can easily swap this for a seed butter like tahini or sunflower seed butter.

Please note that the runny, smooth kind is often best for recipes as it mixes in better:

Peanut butter

Almond butter

Cashew butter

Hazelnut butter

Tahini (made from sesame seeds)

Sunflower seed butter

Baking Essentials

Having a well-stocked cupboard means you can bake anything you like from this book, so here are a few basics I like to always have in:

Flours. A selection of flours will be useful in the long run – I always have plain/all-purpose (and a gluten-free alternative, ensuring to add my own xanthan gum if it doesn't have it in already) and self-raising/self-rising flour. I also use strong white bread flour in my yeasted recipes, as it adds a great texture, and I have buckwheat, spelt, chickpea (gram) and coconut flour at home which are all used throughout this book. I also love using oat flour, but please make your own (see below).

Coconut sugar is the main sugar I use throughout the book as it's unrefined and has a lovely rich caramel-like flavour and colour. You can also swap in golden or regular caster/superfine sugar in these recipes.

Maple or agave syrups are my go-to choices for sticky syrups as they are both plant-based and natural

Fast-action dried yeast is essential for my dough recipes

Rolled oats are a key part

of this book for breakfast and for baking. To make your own oat flour, blend rolled oats in a blender to a fine flour-like texture and store in a sealed container at room temperature for 1–2 months.

Protein powders feature in a few recipes but are not essential. I like to have a good-quality vanilla protein powder and chocolate protein powder to hand, for adding to smoothies and for mixing with thick coconut yogurt to make frostings. Ensure they are gluten-free and nut-free where needed and that they are as additive-free as possible. I love the brand Form Nutrition for this.

Nutritional yeast is important for adding an umami, sometimes cheesy flavour, or for adding richness. This is not to be confused with fast-action dried yeast, and it can be found in most supermarkets.

Spices and Dried Herbs

These are essential for adding flavour to food and for creating the best dining experiences. My most-used spices and dried herbs in the rack are:

Hot smoked and smoked paprika. Both lend a lovely smoky flavour, but note that the difference is that hot smoked paprika also adds fiery heat, whereas regular smoked paprika does not.

Ground cumin

Ground coriander

Ground turmeric

Garam masala

Chilli flakes and/or chilli powder or cayenne pepper

Dried basil

Dried oregano

Dried thyme

Dried rosemary

Ground cinnamon

Ground ginger

Kala namak (aka black sea salt) is a sulphurous powder which has a real "eggy" smell and taste to it. It is not essential but a little goes a long way and it will last for years.

A Few Kitchen Gadgets

Here are a few things you'll find in my kitchen that make these recipes a breeze to make and they're ones you probably already have:

Electricals

High-speed blender (I have a Vitamix) for cheesecake mixes and smoothies

Smaller blender (for sauces)

High-powered food processor (like a Magimix) for blitzing and making hummus

Stand mixer (this is useful for beating buttercream frosting, or you can use an electric hand-held mixer)

Waffle maker (not essential as you can turn the recipe into pancakes)

Toaster/kettle (all kitchen gadgets you have to make your life easier)

Microwave (I use this mainly for melting chocolate and coconut oil)

Kitchen scales (I always recommend using scales to weigh out ingredients instead of cups as they are a lot more accurate, so please use these when you can). I use digital electronic scales and I recommend always working in grams (metric) where possible.

Pots and Pans

Baking pans. I have a selection of 15cm/6in and 20cm/8in round and square baking pans for cakes and bars.

Loaf pan (for banana bread and baking bread)

Non-stick frying pans (look for toxic-free ones); I use a small and large pan throughout

Saucepans in small, medium and large

Enamel bakeware or ceramic dishes (which are ovenproof)

Baking sheets (small and large or use a few small ones)

Mixing bowls in small, medium and large

Ovens and Hobs/ Stovetops

Every oven and hob/stovetop will be different and you will know yours best in terms of how quickly it heats up and how evenly it cooks or bakes, so use the recipe times and heat levels as guides and adjust accordingly.

As a rule, I use the middle shelf of the oven to bake and roast and I turn baking sheets around halfway through the time to ensure they bake evenly. If you are using a fan-assisted oven, you will need to adjust the temperature, too, usually by reducing the standard conventional electric oven temperature by 20°C so, for example, 180°C is 160°C fan-assisted.

The Feel Good Kitchen Week

Here is an example of a week's worth of eating, from breakfast through to lunch, dinner and a snack or dessert for each of two main focuses: Healthy Brain and Happy Mind. Note that you can have leftovers from most recipes, so you can repeat some meals. Remember to pick and choose based on what you have in the refrigerator and what you fancy that day:

Meal / Day	Breakfast	Lunch	Dinner	Snack or Dessert
Monday	Brain Food Granola with coconut yogurt and berries (see page 27)	Kale Caesar Salad with Crispy Tofu (see page 150)	Lentil and Mushroom "Meatballs" with Homemade Tomato Sauce (see page 180)	Snickers-style Protein Bars (see page 98)
Tuesday	High-protein Avocado Toast with Crispy Chickpeas (see page 30)	Sweet Potato Falafel Wraps with Herby Tahini (see page 154)	Golden Miso Curry Noodle Bowls (see page 166)	Cherry Coconut Oat Crumble Slices (see page 189)
Wednesday	Matcha Pistachio Creamy Oats (see page 28)	Avocado, Strawberry and Chickpea Salad (see page 48)	Roasted Carrot and Chickpea Kale Bowls (see page 82)	Dark Chocolate Brazil Nut Flapjacks (see page 186)
Thursday	The Best Three Protein Smoothies (see page 120)	Roasted Vegetable and Salsa Verde Bean Sandwich (see page 52)	Green Goddess Pasta (see page 80)	Sun-dried Tomato and Olive Muffins (see page 104)
Friday	Neapolitan Chia Pudding (see page 116)	Sticky Tofu Halloumi Glow Bowls (see page 158)	Roasted Aubergine and Broccoli Lentil Curry (see page 74)	Dark Chocolate Avocado Pistachio Truffles (see page 96)
Saturday	Scrambled Tofu Hummus Breakfast Bowls (see page 38)	Mexican-inspired Shredded Tofu Tacos (see page 58)	Sweet Potato Pizzas (see page 172)	Hidden Vegetable Chocolate Fudge Cake (see page 106)
Sunday	Strawberry Cheesecake French Toast (see page 132)	Hidden Vegetable Squash and Tomato Soup (see page 144)	One-pan Courgette Lasagne (see page 164)	Sun-dried Tomato Pesto and Spinach Babka (see page 195)

PART 1

healthy brain

CHAPTER 1

breakfast & brunch

Brain Food Granola

Serves 6 (makes approx. 500g/1lb 2oz) | **Prep time:** 10 minutes + cooling | **Cook time:** 25 minutes

This granola is perfect brain food as it's packed with brain-loving nuts and seeds. Variety is key so use your favourite blend of nuts and seeds like walnuts, Brazil nuts and pumpkin seeds alongside omega-3-rich chia seeds and flaxseed. This granola is delicious served with dairy-free milk or coconut yogurt, or I just like to snack on it from the jar!

For the granola

2 tbsp walnut, avocado or coconut oil

80g/2¾oz/⅓ cup runny smooth peanut butter

2 tbsp maple syrup

1 tsp vanilla extract

125g/4½oz/1¼ cups rolled oats

125g/4½oz/1 cup mixed nuts (e.g. walnuts, pecans, hazelnuts, Brazil nuts), chopped

70g/2½oz/½ cup mixed seeds (e.g. sunflower and pumpkin seeds)

2 tbsp hulled hemp seeds

1 tbsp ground flaxseed

1 tbsp chia seeds

1 tsp ground cinnamon

a pinch of salt

1. Preheat the oven to 160°C/320°F/Gas 3 and line a large baking sheet with baking parchment. If using coconut oil, melt this now.

2. Into a large mixing bowl, stir together the peanut butter, maple syrup, the oil and vanilla until smooth. Stir in the oats, mixed nuts, all of the seeds, the cinnamon and salt. Stir to a sticky mix.

3. Pour the granola mix onto the lined baking sheet and pat down with a spoon to make a compact rectangle.

4. Bake in the oven for 25 minutes, turning the baking sheet around every 10 minutes, until golden all over and crisping at the sides. It will smell fragrant and nutty.

5. Allow the granola to cool fully on the baking sheet.

Top Tip

You can also use cashew or almond butter instead of peanut butter. Or make this recipe completely nut-free by using sunflower seed butter or runny smooth tahini instead of peanut butter and swap the nuts for more sunflower and pumpkin seeds.

Matcha Pistachio Creamy Oats

Serves 4 | **Prep time:** 10 minutes

Give your brain a feel-good boost for breakfast with these super green, creamy and delicious blended oats. They are made with simple wholesome ingredients, providing a source of fibre, protein and a gentle caffeine buzz and they will keep you going all morning. The trick is to soak the oats in boiling water to aid digestion and make your tummy happy.

For the oats

360ml/12fl oz/1½ cups water

4 tsp matcha green
    tea powder

200g/7oz/2 cups rolled oats

2 ripe bananas

120g/4¼oz/½ cup thick
    coconut yogurt

120ml/4fl oz/½ cup
    plant-based milk

4 tbsp chia seeds

4 tbsp hulled hemp seeds

2 tbsp runny smooth tahini

2 scoops (approx. 60g/2¼oz
    or 6 tbsp) of vegan
    vanilla protein powder

30g/1oz/¼ cup shelled
    pistachios, chopped

To serve

extra thick coconut yogurt

extra crushed pistachios

4 tbsp pomegranate seeds

4 tbsp runny smooth tahini

1. Boil the water and allow it to cool down slightly so as to not ruin the matcha powder.

2. Add the matcha to a bowl and add some of the hot water to form a paste before slowly whisking in the rest of the water. Now stir in the oats and leave for 5 minutes to soften and swell.

3. Into a small blender, add the soaked matcha oats, the bananas, coconut yogurt, milk, chia seeds, hemp seeds, tahini and protein powder. Blend until really creamy and smooth, stopping to scrape down the sides as necessary.

4. Now stir in the chopped pistachios.

5. Have four glasses or bowls ready and spoon some extra coconut yogurt into each. Spoon in the matcha oat mixture and then top with some more yogurt, some extra crushed pistachios, the pomegranate seeds and extra tahini.

6. Eat straight away, or cover tightly and refrigerate for 2–3 days.

High-protein Avocado Toast
with Crispy Chickpeas

Serves 4 | **Prep time:** 15 minutes | **Cook time:** 20 minutes

Avocado toast is a go-to breakfast for a lot of us, but this version has had a major upgrade in the form of chickpeas/garbanzo beans and peas. Adding both adds lots of protein, as well as fibre (important for gut and brain health), along with an array of vitamins, minerals and antioxidants. Adding a sprinkling of hemp seeds will add omega-3 fatty acids, which support brain health, while avocados are loaded with healthy unsaturated fats that can help to reduce blood pressure and prevent cognitive decline, plus the pink pickles will feed your gut microbiome with friendly bacteria.

For the homemade pink pickles

1 red onion, thinly sliced

½ tsp salt

½ tsp caster/superfine sugar

120ml/4fl oz/½ cup apple cider vinegar or white wine vinegar

For the crispy chickpeas

1 x 400g/14oz can chickpeas/garbanzo beans, drained, rinsed and patted dry (240g/8½oz/1½ cups drained weight)

½ tsp hot smoked paprika

½ tsp ground cumin

1 tbsp olive oil

salt and pepper, to taste

For the smashed avocado

2 large ripe avocados

150g/5½oz/1 cup frozen petit pois, defrosted

juice of 1 lime

a pinch of chilli flakes

1 tbsp nutritional yeast (optional)

To serve

4 large slices of sourdough, or other bread of your choice

4 handfuls of watercress, rocket/arugula or baby spinach

4 heaped tbsp No Nuts Homemade Cream Cheese (see page 198)

4 tbsp hulled hemp seeds

1 spring onion/ scallion, sliced

1. Make the pink pickles first as they need to sit for a bit before serving. Place the onion slices in a medium mixing bowl, then add in the salt, sugar and 1 tbsp of the vinegar and massage with your hands for 1 minute, to soften the onion. Transfer to a clean glass jar and pour over the remaining vinegar, then seal the jar, shake well and allow to sit for 30 minutes before serving. Refrigerate the pink pickles in the sealed jar for up to 2 weeks, ensuring the onion slices are fully submerged in vinegar (adding extra if needed). Use as required (you'll need 4 tbsp for this recipe).

2. Meanwhile, preheat the oven to 200°C/400°F/Gas 6 and line a large baking sheet with baking parchment.

3. For the crispy chickpeas, add the chickpeas to the lined baking sheet with the paprika, cumin, olive oil and some salt and pepper. Toss well, then bake in the oven for 20 minutes, turning the baking sheet around and shaking the chickpeas after 10 minutes.

4. In the meantime, for the smashed avocado, peel, halve and pit the avocados and place on a large plate or chopping board. Add the peas and squeeze over the lime juice. Add the chilli flakes and nutritional yeast (if using) and season with salt and pepper. Use a fork to mash it all together until mainly smooth, with some small chunks.

5. Toast the bread and prepare the other toppings.

6. Place some salad leaves onto four plates and add on the toast slices. Spread with the cream cheese and then spread on the smashed avocado mix. Top with the crispy chickpeas, followed by the hemp seeds, some pink pickles (1 tbsp per serving) and spring onion slices.

7. This is best enjoyed straight away.

Top Tip

You can swap the chickpeas for canned cannellini beans, butter/ lima beans or lentils, too, to make for a crispy topping. Cook them in the same way as above.

Butter Bean and Tofu Feta Shakshuka

Serves 4 | **Prep time:** 10 minutes | **Cook time:** 20 minutes

Shakshuka is a much-loved staple for breakfast or brunch, and this version is not only high in protein thanks to the butter/lima beans, it also has the best homemade salty, tangy tofu "feta" on top. The mix of spices, vegetables and legumes adds a vast range of antioxidants, vitamins and minerals, which all feed our gut microbiome in different ways. Serve with your favourite breads, mixed seeds or whole grains for a filling fibre-packed meal.

For the tofu feta

1 tsp dried oregano

1 tsp dried rosemary

2 garlic cloves, crushed

2 tbsp nutritional yeast

4 tbsp extra virgin olive oil

2 tbsp lemon juice

large pinch salt and pepper

40g/1½oz/¼ cup pitted green olives, sliced

1 x 200g/7oz extra-firm tofu, drained

For the shakshuka beans

1 tbsp olive oil

1 onion, finely diced

1 red pepper, deseeded and finely diced

3 garlic cloves, crushed

1 tsp hot smoked paprika

½ tsp ground coriander

½ tsp ground cumin

180g/6¼oz/1 cup cherry tomatoes, halved

1 tbsp harissa paste

1 x 400g/14oz can butter/lima beans, drained and rinsed (240g/8½oz drained weight)

1 x 400g/14oz can chopped tomatoes

To serve

4 tbsp thick coconut yogurt

handful of fresh coriander/cilantro, chopped

1. Start by preparing the tofu feta. In a container with a lid, stir together the oregano, rosemary, garlic, nutritional yeast, olive oil, lemon juice and the salt and pepper until combined. Now add in the olives and, using your hands, crumble in the tofu in small chunks. Stir it all really well, then cover and leave to one side until needed. You can refrigerate the tofu like this for up to 1 week.

2. For the shakshuka, heat the olive oil in a large, non-stick pan over a medium-high heat, and once hot, add the onion, red pepper and garlic. Fry off for 5 minutes to soften the onion, then add in the paprika, ground coriander and cumin with some salt and pepper. Stir well and fry for 1 minute to release the aromas.

3. Stir in the cherry tomatoes and place a lid on the pan. Cook the tomatoes for 5 minutes to soften, stirring a few times. Roughly smash the tomatoes with the back of a wooden spoon.

4. Now stir in the harissa paste, butter beans, canned tomatoes and 60ml/2fl oz/¼ cup water. Replace the lid on the pan and bubble gently for 10 minutes to warm through.

5. To serve, spoon the shakshuka into bowls and top with some of the tofu feta as well as swirls of coconut yogurt, the coriander and seeds. Serve with your favourite bread or toast.

6. Enjoy straight away, or allow the shakshuka to cool, then refrigerate in a sealed container for 2–3 days. You can also freeze the shakshuka for 1 month. Defrost (if frozen) and warm back up to eat.

Top Tip
You can use any canned beans or legumes for this plant-based shakshuka. I also like cannellini beans or chickpeas/garbanzo beans, or try serving it with rice or roast potatoes for a different meal.

Red Lentil Pancakes
with Black Beans and Avocado

Serves 4 (makes 16 smaller American-style pancakes)
Prep time: 15 minutes + 30 minutes soaking | **Cook time:** 20–30 minutes

These savoury pancakes make a welcome addition to any brunch table. They taste amazing – zingy, creamy, fresh and vibrant with gentle spices and lots of lime – and are also high in fibre, protein and wholefood goodness. They are full of gut-friendly ingredients like apple cider vinegar, hemp seeds and chia seeds, which our brains love thanks to the omega-3 fatty acids. The black bean, tomato and avocado topper also boasts healthy unsaturated fats, which may help to prevent cognitive decline, and the range of different vitamins may help to protect cells from age-related damage. This really is a powerhouse of a brunch to enjoy with family or friends.

For the red lentil pancakes

200g/7oz/1 cup dried split red lentils

320ml/11¼fl oz/2⅓ cups room-temperature water

4 tbsp chickpea/ gram flour, sifted

2 tbsp hulled hemp seeds

1 tsp baking powder

1 tsp apple cider vinegar

½ tsp ground turmeric

½ tsp smoked paprika

olive oil or spray oil, for frying

For the black beans

1 x 400g/14oz can black beans, drained and rinsed (240g/8½oz/1½ cups drained weight)

160g/5¾oz/1 cup cherry tomatoes, cut into quarters

2 spring onions/ scallions, thinly sliced

2 tsp extra virgin olive oil

grated zest and juice of 1 lime

½ red chilli, finely chopped (optional)

salt and pepper, to taste

For the lime yogurt

240g/8½oz/1 cup thick coconut yogurt

juice of 2 limes

¼ tsp ground cumin

To serve

4 handfuls of salad leaves (e.g. rocket/arugula, watercress or spinach)

2 ripe avocados, peeled, pitted and sliced

4 tbsp Homemade Pink Pickles (see page 31)

2 tbsp mixed white and black sesame seeds

a few sprigs of fresh coriander/cilantro leaves

1. Add the red lentils to a medium heatproof bowl and cover with 240ml/8½fl oz/2 cups boiling water. Stir well, then leave to soak and swell for 30 minutes.

2. While the lentils soak, prepare the black bean mix. Add all the ingredients to a bowl with some salt and pepper and stir well. Leave to one side.

3. Also, prepare the lime yogurt by stirring together all the ingredients in a small bowl until smooth, seasoning with salt and pepper.

4. When the lentils are done, drain and rinse them well before adding to a blender with the rest of the pancake ingredients. Blend until smooth, then allow the batter to rest for 5 minutes.

5. Heat a large non-stick frying pan with some oil over a medium-high heat. Once hot, add a few heaped tbsp of the batter into the middle, then spread out into a circle, about the size of your hand (make a couple of pancakes at a time if they will fit). Reduce the heat to medium and fry for 1–2 minutes until bubbles appear on top. Use a spatula to carefully flip the pancake over and cook on the second side for 1–2 minutes more. Place on a plate and cover with a dish towel to keep warm. Repeat to make 16 pancakes in total.

6. To plate up, divide the salad leaves between four plates and top with the red lentil pancakes (4 per serving). Add on spoonfuls of the lime yogurt, the black bean mix, avocado slices, pink pickles and sesame seeds. Finish with the coriander leaves, and enjoy straight away.

7. Refrigerate leftover cooked and cooled pancakes, black beans and lime yogurt separately in sealed containers for 2–3 days and enjoy cold, or warm the pancakes back up in a non-stick pan over a medium heat to serve.

Chocolate Breakfast Mousse Pots

Serves 2 generously; serves 4 as a smaller dessert | **Prep time:** 20 minutes | **Cook time:** 10 minutes

If you fancy chocolate mousse for breakfast, then this is the recipe for you. It is the perfect balance between wholesome goodness and indulgence. This mousse is made from nutrient-rich sweet potato, blended together with naturally sweet dates and banana, raw cacao powder, which is full of brain-supportive minerals such as zinc and magnesium, and gut-healthy coconut yogurt, and it's layered up and topped with homemade caramelized banana slices and nuts. The combination of nuts, fruit and veg is ideal for boosting your brain first thing (or try it in the evening as a dessert).

For the mousse

1 medium sweet potato

2 Medjool dates, pitted

120g/4¼oz/½ cup thick coconut yogurt

25g/1oz/¼ cup raw cacao powder

1 ripe banana

2 tbsp runny smooth peanut butter

1 tsp vanilla extract

a pinch of salt

For the caramelized bananas and nuts

1 tbsp maple syrup

½ tbsp walnut, avocado or olive oil

1 ripe banana, sliced into coins

30g/1oz/¼ cup blanched hazelnuts, roughly chopped

To serve

2–4 tbsp thick coconut yogurt (optional)

2–4 tbsp runny smooth peanut butter (optional)

1 tbsp chopped dark/ bittersweet chocolate

1. Start by preparing the sweet potato. Stab it all over and microwave on High for about 5 minutes, turning the potato every minute, or until soft in the middle. Allow to cool until it's easy to handle. Carefully peel away the skin (you can eat this!) and leave the potato flesh to cool completely, then mash it up. You will have about 150g/5½oz/¾ cup of sweet potato mash.

2. If the dates are quite hard, soak them in boiling water for 10 minutes and then drain.

3. To make the mousse, add the sweet potato, dates and all the remaining ingredients to a blender and blend until really smooth and creamy.

4. Refrigerate the mousse while you make the caramelized bananas and nuts.

5. Add the maple syrup and oil to a non-stick frying pan and allow to just bubble, stirring often. Now add all the banana slices, ensuring they don't overlap. Cook over a medium-high heat for 3–5 minutes until golden underneath, then carefully flip them over and cook on the second side for about 2 minutes until golden. Remove from the pan to a plate. Using the same pan, add the hazelnuts to the remaining syrup mix and cook for 1–2 minutes to coat the nuts. Remove from the pan.

6. To serve, divide the chocolate mousse between two or four glasses, adding some extra coconut yogurt and/or peanut butter, if you like, the caramelized bananas and nuts and the dark chocolate.

7. Enjoy straight away, or cover tightly and refrigerate for 2–3 days.

Top Tips

You can use pumpkin purée instead of the sweet potato, and make these nut-free by using runny smooth tahini instead of peanut butter, use avocado or olive oil and swap the hazelnuts for sunflower seeds.

Scrambled Tofu Hummus Breakfast Bowls

Serves 4 | **Prep time:** 15 minutes + 10 minutes marinating | **Cook time:** 20 minutes

These breakfast (or brunch) bowls have all my favourite morning foods in them. They're bursting with good-for-you ingredients, wholefood staples and an abundance of plants. These will ultimately fuel your brain all day long thanks to a few main components: the monounsaturated fats in avocado can help to promote healthy blood flow and prevent cognitive decline; and leafy greens and juicy tomatoes are known for their antioxidant properties which help support your memory. Enjoy these with some hummus, your favourite rye or sourdough bread and a cup of coffee.

For the mushrooms and tomatoes

300g/10½oz/3 cups baby chestnut mushrooms or similar

1½ tbsp olive oil

1 tbsp tamari soy sauce

2 garlic cloves, crushed

4 small vines of cherry tomatoes (approx. 20 tomatoes in total)

salt and pepper, to taste

For the tofu scramble

2 x 200g/7oz blocks of extra-firm tofu, drained

120ml/4fl oz/½ cup plant-based milk

2 tbsp runny smooth tahini

2 tbsp nutritional yeast

½ tsp smoked paprika

½ tsp garlic granules

½ tsp onion powder

¼ tsp ground turmeric

¼ tsp kala namak black salt (optional) (see Top Tip)

1 tbsp olive oil

For the bowls

4 large handfuls of salad leaves (e.g. a mix of baby spinach, watercress and rocket/arugula)

8 tbsp Homemade Hummus (see page 159)

2 ripe avocados, peeled, pitted and halved

2 spring onions/ scallions, thinly sliced

4 tbsp mixed white and black sesame seeds

2 sprigs of fresh coriander/ cilantro, leaves only

4 slices of rye, sourdough or wholemeal/whole-wheat bread, toasted

1. Scrub the mushrooms clean, then add to a large bowl with 1 tbsp of the olive oil, the tamari, garlic and some salt and pepper and toss well. Leave to marinate for 10 minutes.

2. Preheat the oven to 180°C/350°F/Gas 4 and line a large baking sheet with baking parchment.

3. When the mushrooms are marinated, scoop them onto the lined baking sheet (leave any marinade in the bowl) and lay the tomatoes next to them. Drizzle the tomatoes with the remaining ½ tbsp of olive oil and season with salt and pepper. Bake in the oven for 20 minutes, turning the baking sheet around halfway through.

4. Add the salad leaves to the marinade bowl and toss well to absorb any leftover flavour.

5. When the vegetables have 10 minutes left, prepare the tofu scramble. Crumble the tofu between your fingers into some small and some larger pieces on a plate or board. In a small bowl, whisk together all the remaining ingredients, except the olive oil, until smooth, adding some salt and pepper.

6. Heat a large, non-stick frying pan with the olive oil, and once hot, add in the crumbled tofu. Stir over a medium-high heat for 1 minute, then pour in the milky mix and cook for 3–5 minutes, stirring regularly, until the liquid has been mostly absorbed and the tofu is "wet".

7. Divide the salad leaves between four bowls and top with the tofu scramble, roasted mushrooms and tomatoes, hummus and avocado. Sprinkle over the spring onions, sesame seeds and coriander leaves and serve with your favourite toasted bread. This is best enjoyed straight away.

Top Tip

The kala namak is a unique sulphurous black salt that adds a very "eggy" smell and taste to this scrambled tofu and a little goes a long way. It's not essential, so you can leave it out, but I recommend trying it!

Brain Booster Creamy Oats Three Ways

Serves 4 using the oats base, plus one of the toppings (each topping serves 4)
Prep time: 15 minutes | **Cook time:** 10–25 minutes

Porridge/oatmeal is one of the best ways to start the day. The oats provide a slow release of energy, keeping you satiated and fuelling your brain. The chia and hemp add omega-3 fatty acid goodness, while the buckwheat adds wholegrain fibre to support a healthy gut. The diversity in the toppings adds healthful fats, antioxidants and a variety of vitamins and minerals, which are all important for brain cognition.

For the oat base

200g/7oz/2 cups rolled oats

4 tbsp chia seeds

4 tbsp hulled hemp seeds

4 tbsp buckwheat groats

960ml/34fl oz/4 cups plant-based milk, plus extra

4 tbsp thick coconut yogurt

For the rhubarb and ginger

3 rhubarb stalks, trimmed and cut into small chunks (approx. 260g/9¼oz/2 cups trimmed weight)

1 tbsp coconut sugar

1 tbsp lemon juice

½ tsp ground ginger

4 tbsp crushed pecans

4 tbsp pomegranate seeds

For the cherry bakewell

8 tbsp almond butter

1 tsp vanilla extract

160g/5¾oz/2 heaped cups frozen (pitted) cherries

1 tbsp coconut sugar

4 tbsp flaked/sliced almonds

For the cacao pistachio

4 tbsp raw cacao powder, sifted

2 tbsp maple syrup, plus extra

4 tbsp crushed pistachios

4 tbsp dark/bittersweet chocolate chips

1. Make the brain booster oats base by adding the oats, chia seeds, hemp seeds, buckwheat groats and measured milk into a large saucepan, stir, then leave to soak for 10 minutes while you prepare the toppings.

2. For the rhubarb and ginger porridge, preheat the oven to 180°C/350°F/Gas 4. Add the rhubarb chunks to an ovenproof dish with the coconut sugar, lemon juice and ginger. Toss well, then bake for 25 minutes, stirring every 10 minutes. With 10 minutes left, cook the porridge (soaked oats base) over a medium heat, stirring often, for about 7–8 minutes until creamy. Add more milk if you prefer it runnier. Pour into four bowls, top each portion with 1 tbsp of coconut yogurt, the roasted rhubarb, pecans and pomegranate seeds. Pour over any extra rhubarb juices.

3. For the cherry bakewell porridge, add 4 tbsp of the almond butter to the saucepan of soaked oats with the vanilla and cook as above, then add more milk, if needed. Meanwhile, add the frozen cherries to a small heatproof bowl with the coconut sugar, then warm through in the microwave on High for 30–60 seconds, stirring once, until glossy and sticky. Divide the porridge between four bowls, top each portion with 1 tbsp of coconut yogurt, 1 tbsp of the remaining almond butter, the cherries and flaked almonds.

4. For the cacao pistachio porridge, add the cacao powder and maple syrup to the saucepan of soaked oats and cook as above, then add more milk, if needed. Pour into four bowls, topping each with 1 tbsp of coconut yogurt, crushed pistachios and chocolate chips. Drizzle with maple syrup.

5. All of these oats are best enjoyed straight away.

Top Tip

If you don't have a waffle machine, you can make these as pancakes. Follow the recipe above, then add spoonfuls of batter to a large, non-stick frying pan lightly greased with olive oil and cook over a medium-high heat for 2–3 minutes on each side, until golden. Serve as above.

Chickpea Flour Savoury Waffles
with Tomatoes and Avocado Salsa

Serves 4 (makes 8 small waffles) | **Prep time:** 15 minutes | **Cook time:** 15 minutes

For the savoury waffles

200g/7oz/2 cups
  chickpea (gram) flour

2 tbsp nutritional yeast

½ tsp baking powder

½ tsp hot smoked paprika

¼ tsp ground turmeric

240ml/8½fl oz/1 cup
  plant-based milk

2 tsp apple cider vinegar

2 spring onions/
  scallions, thinly sliced

1 red pepper, deseeded
  and cut into small dice

2 garlic cloves, crushed

1 tbsp chopped fresh herbs
  (e.g. mint, chives and/
  or coriander/cilantro)

60g/2¼oz/2 cups baby
  spinach, finely chopped

olive oil, for greasing

salt and pepper, to taste

For the salsa

160g/5¾oz/1 cup cherry
  tomatoes, finely chopped

1 ripe avocado, peeled,
  pitted and finely chopped

juice of 1 lime

1 tbsp chopped fresh
  coriander/cilantro

For the tahini yogurt

4 tbsp runny smooth tahini

4 tbsp thick coconut yogurt

2 tsp lemon juice

2 tsp tamari soy sauce

2 tbsp plant-based milk

To serve

4 handfuls of salad leaves

Savoury waffles are one of the best brunch dishes when you fancy something fresh, healthful and satisfying, and the base of chickpea (gram) flour makes these waffles high-fibre, high-protein and naturally gluten-free. They are full of gut-healthy ingredients like apple cider vinegar and fermented yogurt to feed our gut microbiome, while the monounsaturated fats in the avocado work to reduce blood pressure and prevent cognitive decline.

1. For the waffle batter, whisk together the chickpea flour, nutritional yeast, baking powder, paprika, turmeric and some salt and pepper in a large mixing bowl. Now whisk in the milk and vinegar and leave to stand for 5 minutes. Once the batter is rested, stir in the spring onions, red pepper, garlic, herbs and baby spinach.

2. Lightly grease the waffle machine with olive oil and allow it to heat up. Once hot, use a large spoon to fill the waffle irons with the batter and then cook according to the manufacturer's instructions. The waffles will be golden and slightly crispy on top when they are ready. Remove the waffles and keep them warm in a low oven. Repeat to make all the waffles (you'll make 8 in total).

4. While the waffles are cooking, stir together all of the salsa ingredients in a small bowl.

5. Also, make the tahini yogurt by whisking together all the ingredients in a separate small bowl and seasoning with salt and pepper.

6. To serve, add some salad leaves to your plates and top with the waffles and salsa, then spoon over tahini yoghurt. Add a lime wedge to each portion, if you like, and enjoy.

7. Refrigerate all the components separately in sealed containers for 2–3 days and enjoy warmed back up or cold.

Grain-free High-protein Bircher Muesli

Serves 4 | **Prep time:** 10 minutes + overnight soaking

This high-protein Bircher muesli contains no oats or grains, but is packed with nutritious ingredients including a variety of seeds and buckwheat (which is actually a seed), giving your brain a healthy boost of omegas, healthy fats, fibre and antioxidants. This recipe is also bursting with gut-healthy fermented coconut yogurt to support the gut-brain axis thanks to the live bacteria it contains. It's creamy and thick and tastes so delicious topped with fresh berries.

For the Bircher muesli

68g/2½oz/⅓ cup raw buckwheat groats

33g/1oz/⅓ cup vegan protein powder

4 tbsp ground flaxseed

4 tbsp chia seeds

3 tbsp hulled hemp seeds

3 tbsp sunflower seeds

3 tbsp cacao nibs

1 tsp ground cinnamon

160g/5¾oz/⅔ cup thick coconut yogurt

480ml/17fl oz/2 cups plant-based milk

To serve

a handful of fresh berries of your choice, per serving

1 tbsp thick coconut yogurt, per serving

maple syrup (optional)

extra seeds of your choice (optional)

1. Into a large mixing bowl, stir together the buckwheat groats, protein powder, all the seeds, the cacao nibs and cinnamon. Now pour in the yogurt and milk and stir really well until fully incorporated.

2. Leave the mixture for 10 minutes and give it another stir, then if you have the time, repeat this one or two more times. This makes the mixture even creamier.

3. Divide the mixture between four jars or bowls, cover well and refrigerate for 6–8 hours or overnight.

4. When ready to serve, add on your desired toppings and enjoy this Bircher muesli. It will keep refrigerated in the covered jars/bowls for 2–3 days.

Top Tip

Feel free to play around with other seeds and flavours. Try swapping the sunflower seeds for pumpkin seeds and swap the cinnamon for chai spices or ground ginger.

CHAPTER 2

lunch

Avocado, Strawberry and Chickpea Salad

Serves 4 | **Prep time:** 10 minutes | **Cook time:** 20 minutes

This rainbow bowl makes me so happy. Packed with an array of colours, plant-based protein, fibre and vitamins and minerals, it's the perfect nourishing bowl and comes together in around 30 minutes. This brain-boosting lunch is ideal to meal prep or to enjoy as a picnic in the summer.

For the chickpeas

1 x 400g/14oz can chickpeas/garbanzo beans (240g/8½oz/1½ cups drained weight)

¾ tsp hot smoked paprika

½ tsp ground cumin

½ tbsp olive oil

salt and pepper, to taste

For the salad

140g/5oz/1 cup spelt (or other whole grain)

50g/1¾oz/2 cups cavolo nero or kale

60g/2¼oz/2 cups baby spinach

200g/7oz/1 cup fresh strawberries, sliced

2 ripe avocados, peeled, pitted and chopped

60g/2¼oz/½ cup whole almonds (skin on), roughly chopped

a handful of fresh mint and/or parsley, roughly chopped

Homemade Pink Pickles (see page 31)

Tofu Feta (see page 32)

For the dressing

2 tbsp extra virgin olive oil

2 tbsp lemon juice

2 tbsp balsamic vinegar

1 tbsp maple syrup

1 tsp Dijon mustard

1. Start by roasting the chickpeas. Preheat the oven to 180°C/350°F/Gas 4 and line a large baking sheet with baking parchment.

2. Drain and rinse the chickpeas, then pat them dry and spread out on the lined baking sheet. Sprinkle over both spices, some salt and pepper and the olive oil and rub in. Roast in the oven for 20 minutes, tossing the chickpeas after 10 minutes, until crispy and fragrant.

3. Meanwhile, cook the spelt (or other grain of your choice) for the salad, according to the package directions, then leave to one side.

4. For the dressing, whisk together all the ingredients in a small bowl with some salt and pepper until combined.

5. De-stem the kale and roughly chop. Add to a large bowl with 1 tbsp of the dressing and massage with your hands to wilt the leaves. Now add the spinach and toss through.

6. To plate up, divide the kale/spinach mixture between four bowls. Top with some spelt (or other grain), the crispy chickpeas, the strawberries, avocado, almonds, fresh herbs, some pink pickles and tofu feta. Drizzle over the remaining dressing and toss before eating.

7. Refrigerate leftovers in a sealed container for 2–3 days.

Top Tip
Use a gluten-free grain where needed, like buckwheat, quinoa or brown rice.

White Bean and Kale Soup

Serves 4 as a main, serves 6 as a starter or small plate | **Prep time:** 5 minutes | **Cook time:** 25 minutes

Nothing beats a warming bowl of soup and this nourishing recipe is loaded with brain-boosting antioxidants from the kale and fresh vegetables, as well as lots of fibre and protein from the beans. This soup is perfect for all the family or to enjoy with friends and is ideal to prepare ahead of time and warm back up, served with the best giant crunchy golden croutons.

For the soup

1 tbsp olive oil

1 onion, cut into small dice

4 garlic cloves, crushed

1 carrot, washed and finely chopped

a pinch of salt

1 courgette/zucchini, cut into ¼-moon slices

½ tsp dried thyme

½ tsp dried oregano

½ tsp dried basil

¼ tsp chilli flakes

1 tbsp balsamic vinegar

1 x 400g/14oz can chopped tomatoes

2 tbsp tomato purée/paste

2 x 400g/14oz cans cannellini beans, drained and rinsed (480g/1lb 1oz/ 3 cups drained weight)

480–600ml/17–20fl oz/2–2½ cups vegetable stock

50g/1¾oz/2 cups cavolo nero or kale (de-stemmed weight), chopped

2 sprigs of fresh basil

salt and pepper, to taste

For the croutons

4 thick slices of your favourite bread

2 tbsp olive oil

1. Heat the olive oil for the soup in a large non-stick saucepan over a medium heat and fry off the onion, garlic and carrot with the pinch of salt. Cook for 5 minutes until soft, then add the courgette, all the dried herbs and the chilli flakes. Allow to fry off for a further 5 minutes, to soften the vegetables. Season with salt and pepper.

2. Pour in the balsamic vinegar and stir well to de-glaze.

3. Now pour in the chopped tomatoes and add the tomato purée, cannellini beans and vegetable stock. Stir well and bring to a gentle simmer. Cook with a lid on for 15 minutes, stirring occasionally, adding more stock if needed.

4. Meanwhile, make the croutons. Preheat the oven to 180°C/350°F/Gas 4 and line a large baking sheet with baking parchment.

5. Chop the bread into large cubes and spread out on the lined baking sheet, tossing with the olive oil and a little salt. Bake in the oven for 15 minutes, tossing halfway through, until golden and crisp.

6. After the soup has cooked for 15 minutes, transfer half to a mixing bowl and blend with a hand-held/immersion blender until smooth. Return the soup to the pan. Stir in the kale and torn basil sprigs and allow to wilt for 5 minutes.

7. To serve, ladle the soup between bowls and top with some croutons.

8. Enjoy straight away, or refrigerate any cooled leftover soup (minus the croutons) in a sealed container for 2–3 days, or freeze for 1 month, then defrost (if frozen) and warm back up to eat. Keep the cooled croutons in a separate sealed container for 2–3 days.

Top Tip
You can use any canned beans for this recipe such as butter/lima beans or even chickpeas/garbanzo beans.

Roasted Vegetable and Salsa Verde Bean Sandwich

Serves 4 | **Prep time:** 20 minutes | **Cook time:** 25 minutes

This is my new favourite sandwich; it has so many delicious components that come together for one brain-boosting and fuelling meal. The sandwich starts with herby vegetables which contain a host of antioxidants that can support our brain cells to regenerate. The butter/lima beans add important protein and fibre to keep our brains going all day, while the salsa verde is packed with monounsaturated fatty acids to reduce stress on the body, plus fresh leafy greens, which contain a host of nutrients to support brain function.

For the roasted vegetables

2 red onions, cut into small chunks

2 courgettes/zucchini, cut into 1cm/½in-thick slices

2 red peppers, deseeded and cut into thick slices

2 garlic cloves, left whole

2 tbsp olive oil

2 tbsp balsamic vinegar

1 tsp dried mixed herbs

salt and pepper, to taste

For the salsa verde beans

a large handful of fresh coriander/cilantro, leaves and small stalks

a large handful of fresh basil, leaves and small stalks

3 sprigs of fresh mint, leaves only

3 tbsp extra virgin olive oil

2 tbsp runny smooth tahini

2 tbsp lemon juice

½ tbsp capers in brine, drained

½ tsp Dijon mustard

1 x 400g/14oz can butter/lima beans, drained and rinsed (240g/8½oz/1½ cups drained weight)

For the sandwiches

8 slices of sourdough bread, or other bread of your choice

4 tbsp Homemade Hummus (see page 159)

4 handfuls of salad greens (e.g. rocket/arugula or watercress)

2 tbsp hulled hemp seeds

1. Start by preparing the roasted vegetables. Preheat the oven to 200°C/400°F/Gas 6 and line a large baking sheet with baking parchment.

2. Add the onions, courgettes, red peppers and garlic to the lined baking sheet with the olive oil, balsamic vinegar, dried herbs and some salt and pepper and toss well. Arrange the vegetables so they don't overlap, then bake in the oven for 25 minutes, turning the vegetables over after 15 minutes so they cook evenly. They will be soft and starting to char.

3. Remove the garlic from the baking sheet and squeeze the garlic cloves out of their skins into a small blender. Add in all the fresh herbs for the salsa verde, as well as the olive oil, tahini, lemon juice, capers and Dijon mustard and season with salt and pepper. Blend until smooth.

4. Add the drained beans to a medium bowl and lightly mash with a fork to break them down into smaller chunks. Pour in the salsa verde and toss well.

5. Toast the bread for the sandwiches. Spread one slice of toast for each sandwich with the hummus. Top with a selection of roasted vegetables and some salad leaves. Spoon the salsa verde beans on top, sprinkle with the hemp seeds, then sandwich together with a second slice of toast. Slice in half and enjoy.

6. These sandwiches are best enjoyed straight away, or leave to cool, then refrigerate in a sealed container to enjoy later the same day. To prepare the sandwiches for future days, cool and refrigerate the roasted vegetables and salsa verde in separate containers for 2–3 days, and then make up the sandwiches fresh.

Top Tip

You can try other vegetables to roast, like aubergine/eggplant instead of courgette, or orange or yellow pepper instead of red. Thin slices of roasted butternut squash would also be delicious.

Moroccan-inspired Roasted Cauliflower Salad

Serves 4 | **Prep time:** 10 minutes | **Cook time:** 30 minutes

The array of vegetables, chickpeas/garbanzo beans and nuts in this dish will fuel your brain with so much goodness. Chickpeas are a great source of choline, which plays a key role in brain function, as well as magnesium which is essential for healthy nerve function. The flavours are inspired by my love for Moroccan food: the cauliflower is warming, smoky and spicy, while the wholegrain salad with leafy greens, Medjool dates and fresh herbs is so fresh. I love to add lots of homemade hazelnut dukkah on top (which is a staple for sprinkling over any salad) for some nutritious crunch. Plus, nuts and seeds contain tryptophan, which is needed for our body to make serotonin (the happy hormone!)

Top Tips
Use leftover chickpeas in salads or add to the High-protein Avocado Toast with Crispy Chickpeas (see page 30). Use any whole grain you like, for example quinoa, buckwheat, wholemeal/whole-wheat couscous or brown rice, ensuring it's gluten-free where needed.

For the dukkah

45g/1½oz/¼ cup
  blanched hazelnuts

2 tbsp mixed seeds (e.g.
  sunflower, pumpkin etc.)

½ tbsp fennel seeds

½ tbsp cumin seeds

For the roasted cauliflower

1 whole head of cauliflower

1½ x 400g/14oz cans
  chickpeas/garbanzo
  beans, drained,
  rinsed and patted dry
  (360g/12¾oz/2¼ cups
  drained weight)

1 tsp hot smoked paprika

1 tsp ground cumin

½ tsp ground turmeric

½ tsp ground cinnamon

2 tbsp olive oil

salt and pepper, to taste

For the salad

140g/5oz/1 cup spelt (or
  other whole grain)

50g/1¾oz/2 cups
  kale (de-stemmed
  weight), chopped

100g/3½oz/½ cup Brussels
  sprouts, shredded

a pinch of salt

4 Medjool dates, pitted
  and chopped

60g/2¼oz/½ cup
  pomegranate seeds

2 tbsp chopped fresh
  coriander/cilantro

2 tbsp chopped fresh mint

For the dressing

2 tbsp extra virgin olive oil

1 tbsp lemon juice

1 tbsp apple cider vinegar

1 tbsp maple syrup

1 tsp Dijon mustard

a thumb-size piece of root
  ginger, peeled and grated

1. Preheat the oven to 180°C/350°F/Gas 4.

2. For the dukkah, add the hazelnuts and all the seeds to a baking sheet and roast in the oven for 10 minutes until smelling fragrant. Allow to cool briefly, then blitz in a small blender until crumbly with some large and some smaller pieces. This can be made ahead of time and kept in a sealed container at room temperature for 1 month.

2. Prepare the cauliflower. Preheat the oven to 180°C/350°F/Gas 4 (if you've made the dukkah in advance) or keep the oven on. Line two large baking sheets with baking parchment. Trim the leaves from the head of cauliflower, keeping the leaves to one side. Chop the cauliflower head into florets – you will have about 400–500g/14oz–1lb 2oz/3 heaped cups.

4. Add the cauliflower florets, chickpeas, all the spices, the olive oil and some salt and pepper to a large mixing bowl and toss together well. Pour onto one lined baking sheet and roast in the oven for 30 minutes until tender and turning crispy. Stir the mixture halfway through.

5. Add the cauliflower leaves to the same bowl and toss to coat in any leftover seasoning. Add to the second lined baking sheet and roast alongside the cauliflower florets mixture for the final 10 minutes of the cooking time.

6. Meanwhile, cook the spelt (or other grain of your choice) for the salad according to the package directions.

7. Add the kale to a large mixing bowl with the shredded sprouts. Add the pinch of salt and massage with your hands to wilt the leaves.

8. Add the dates to the salad with the pomegranate seeds and fresh herbs.

9. Make the dressing by whisking together the ingredients in a small bowl and seasoning with salt and pepper.

10. Finish off the salad by adding in the cooked spelt (or other grain) and most of the dressing and toss well.

11. Divide the salad between four serving plates, topping with the roasted cauliflower and chickpeas, crispy cauliflower leaves and the rest of the dressing. Sprinkle over the dukkah, and enjoy. The salad can be refrigerated in a sealed container for 2–3 days.

Nutty Orange Brain-food Slaw with Smoky Walnuts

Serves 4 | **Prep time:** 15 minutes | **Cook time:** 8 minutes

I just love a big plate of this brain-food slaw, as it's fresh, vibrant and packed with flavour and texture, while the array of dark leafy greens, fibre-rich chickpeas/garbanzo beans and nuts feed the brain with every bite. The dressing is light and citrussy and works so well with the smoky, slightly spiced walnuts. Serve with some whole grains for a more filling meal, if you like.

For the smoky walnuts

50g/1¾oz/½ cup
  walnut halves

½ tsp hot smoked paprika

¼ tsp chilli flakes

½ tbsp tamari soy sauce

½ tbsp maple syrup

salt and pepper, to taste

For the dressing

3 tbsp extra virgin olive oil

1 tbsp apple cider vinegar

grated zest and juice
  of ½ orange

For the slaw

50g/1¾oz/2 cups
  cavolo nero or kale

1 fennel bulb (approx.
  200g/7oz/2 cups)

¼ head red cabbage
  (approx. 200g/7oz/2 cups)

2 oranges

2 tbsp chopped fresh mint

2 tbsp chopped fresh
  coriander/cilantro

1 x 400g/14oz can
  chickpeas/garbanzo
  beans, drained and
  rinsed (240g/8½oz/1½
  cups drained weight)

1 ripe avocado, sliced

60g/2¼oz/½ cup
  pomegranate seeds

1. Prepare the smoky walnuts first. Preheat the oven to 180°C/350°F/Gas 4. Line a baking sheet with baking parchment.

2. Add all the ingredients for the smoky walnuts into a small bowl. Toss well, then transfer the nuts to the lined baking sheet, leaving the extra sauce behind in the bowl. Bake in the oven for 8 minutes, turning the baking sheet around halfway through – they will smell fragrant when ready. Set aside to cool.

3. Using the same bowl with the leftover sauce, add all of the dressing ingredients and whisk well. Season with salt and pepper.

4. For the slaw, de-stem and finely chop the kale, as well as shredding or thinly slicing the fennel (I like to use a mandoline but this can also be done with a knife) and the cabbage. Peel the oranges and chop the segments into small chunks. Add the kale to a large mixing bowl and add 1 tbsp of the dressing. Massage with your hands for 30 seconds or so to wilt the leaves.

5. Add the other slaw ingredients to the same bowl with half the dressing and toss well to coat.

6. Plate up the salad and top with the smoky walnuts before pouring over the rest of the dressing.

7. Enjoy straight away, or refrigerate in a sealed container for 2–3 days.

Top Tip
Enjoy this salad as it is or serve with the Sweet Potato Falafel on page 154, some hummus and homemade breads as part of a mezze feast.

Mexican-inspired Shredded Tofu Tacos

Serves 4 (enough for 12 small or 8 regular tacos) | **Prep time:** 20 minutes | **Cook time:** 15 minutes

Tacos or tortilla wraps are one of my favourite ways to enjoy Mexican-inspired foods and these superfood tacos are loaded with plant-based protein, fibre, vitamins and minerals, while being really easy to make. They are packed with spices, zingy lime and fresh cooling guacamole, which is great news as avocado contains monounsaturated fats which promote healthy blood flow around the body. The whipped tahini dressing is creamy and slightly "sour" and is high in omega-3 fatty acids – important for improving memory function and great for the skin. These feel-good tacos are perfect for meal-prep lunches or having friends over.

For the tofu

2 x 200g/7oz blocks
  extra-firm tofu, drained
2 tsp hot smoked paprika
1 tsp ground cumin
1 tsp ground coriander
4 tbsp tomato purée/paste
2 tbsp tamari soy sauce
2 tbsp maple syrup
2 tsp olive oil
2 garlic cloves, crushed
salt and pepper, to taste

For the guacamole

2 large ripe avocados
1 red onion, finely chopped
2 tbsp chopped fresh
  coriander/cilantro
juice of 2 limes

For the pickled cabbage

¼ red cabbage,
  shredded (approx.
  150g/5½oz/1½ cups)
½ red onion, finely chopped
juice of ½ lime

For the tomato salsa

80g/2¾oz/½ cup cherry
  tomatoes, finely chopped
½ red onion, finely chopped
juice of ½ lime
2 tbsp chopped fresh
  coriander/cilantro

For the whipped tahini

4 tbsp runny smooth tahini
1 tbsp thick coconut yogurt
juice of 1 lime

To serve

12 small or 8 regular (corn
  or soft flour) tortillas
4 handfuls of salad
  leaves (e.g. rocket/
  arugula or spinach)
1 spring onion/scallion, sliced
1 red chilli, thinly sliced

1. Start by preparing the shredded tofu. Preheat the oven to 180°C/350°F/Gas 4 and line a large baking sheet with baking parchment.

2. Use a box grater to grate the tofu into a large mixing bowl and toss with the paprika, cumin and ground coriander. Season with salt and pepper, then lay out on the lined baking sheet. Bake in the oven for 15 minutes, tossing halfway through. The tofu will be starting to crisp.

3. In the same mixing bowl, stir together all the remaining ingredients. Now pour the baked shredded tofu into the bowl and mix really well.

4. While the tofu bakes, make the guacamole. Add everything to a medium bowl and mash together with a fork. Season with salt and pepper.

5. Also, prepare the quick pickled cabbage. Add everything to another bowl with a pinch of salt and massage with your hands for 30 seconds to soften the cabbage and onion.

6. For the tomato salsa, stir everything together in a small bowl and season with salt and pepper.

7. Finally, prepare the whipped tahini while the tofu is still baking, by whisking together the tahini, yogurt, lime juice and some salt and pepper until thick, then slowly add in enough water (about 1 –2 tbsp) to reach a pourable consistency.

8. To serve the tacos, lay out the tortillas, then add some salad leaves to each, followed by some quick pickled cabbage, the shredded tofu, some guacamole, tomato salsa and a drizzle of whipped tahini. Finish with the spring onion and chilli slices, and enjoy.

9. Once made, these tacos are best eaten straight away, but you can refrigerate all the components separately in sealed containers for 2–3 days, then make your tacos when you are ready.

Top Tips

The ingredients list may seem long, but there are a lot of repeats: limes, red onions and fresh coriander are in abundance, so read the recipe before starting. Feel free to add extra veggies to these tacos, like red pepper in the salsa or sliced cucumber into the tortillas.

Spinach Lentil Fritters with Herby Yogurt

Serves 4 | **Prep time:** 15 minutes | **Cook time:** 20 minutes

These high-protein fritters make a delicious quick and easy lunch. They're packed with dark leafy greens, which can help to boost your brain function and aid memory. The healthy monounsaturated and polyunsaturated fats in the tahini are great for nourishing your body, while the fermented coconut yogurt, extra seeds, avocado and pink pickles will feed your gut bacteria and add so much diversity to your plate – and we all know that good gut health supports good mental health, too! I also love to enjoy these the next day in a packed lunch, as they are equally delicious cold.

For the fritters

200g/7oz/1 cup dried
  split red lentils

240ml/8½fl oz/1 cup water

1 tsp brown rice miso paste

2 tbsp olive oil

2 spring onions/scallions,
  finely chopped

2 garlic cloves, crushed

½ red chilli, finely chopped

1 tsp hot smoked paprika

1 tsp ground cumin

120g/4¼oz/4 cups baby
  spinach, chopped

80g/2¾oz/½ cup
  chickpea (gram) flour

4 tbsp nutritional yeast

2 tbsp ground flaxseed

salt and pepper, to taste

For the herby yogurt

240g/8½oz/1 cup thick
  coconut yogurt

4 tbsp runny smooth tahini

grated zest and
  juice of 1 lime

4 tbsp chopped fresh mixed
  herbs (e.g. mint, chives
  and coriander/cilantro)

To serve

4 handfuls of rocket/arugula

4 tbsp mixed seeds
  of your choice

4 tbsp Homemade Pink
  Pickles (see page 31)

1 avocado, peeled,
  pitted and cubed

1. Start by cooking the lentils. Add the lentils, water and miso paste to a small saucepan and bring just to the boil. Reduce the heat, cover and simmer over a low heat for 10 minutes until all the water has been absorbed.

2. Meanwhile, heat 1 tbsp of the olive oil in a large non-stick frying pan over a medium heat, add the spring onions, garlic and chilli and fry off for 3–4 minutes until softening. Add the paprika and cumin with some salt and pepper and fry for 1 minute until fragrant. Now add the spinach and sauté until it has wilted and is darker in colour.

3. To make the fritter batter, add the cooked lentils, the spinach mix, the chickpea flour, nutritional yeast and ground flaxseed to a large mixing bowl and stir well to mix. Leave for 5 minutes to thicken.

4. Scoop out large tablespoonfuls of the batter and gently roll into rounds – the mixture will be wet and sticky. Heat a little of the remaining olive oil in the same frying pan (no need to rinse it) over a medium-high heat, and once hot, add in the fritters. You will make 12 fritters and will need to fry them in batches. Cook each batch for 3–4 minutes, until the fritters are golden brown on the underside, then carefully flip over to cook on the second side for 2 minutes until golden brown. Remove the cooked fritters from the pan and keep warm on a covered plate.

5. To make the herby yogurt, stir together all the ingredients until smooth and season to taste with salt and pepper.

6. To serve the fritters, spread some of the herby yogurt onto each plate, top with some of the fritters, then add the rocket, some seeds, pink pickles and avocado.

7. Enjoy straight away, or once cool, refrigerate the fritters and yogurt in separate containers for 2–3 days. The fritters can also be frozen for 1 month. Defrost before enjoying warm (reheated) or cold.

Top Tip

You can add other flavours (instead of the paprika and cumin) to these fritters like ½ tsp of ground turmeric and a pinch of cayenne pepper, or try ½ tsp of dried oregano and ½ tsp of dried basil.

Roasted Squash and Tofu Sprout Salad

Serves 4 | **Prep time:** 20 minutes | **Cook time:** 30 minutes

This vibrant, wholesome and nourishing salad is loaded with antioxidants from the array of vegetables, whole grains and nuts it contains. The chilli-roasted squash and red onion pair perfectly with the smoked tofu cubes (great for adding protein) and the quinoa sprout slaw is crunchy, fresh and tossed in a zingy dressing. All these wholefoods can help to boost brain function, improve memory and protect it from excess stress. This salad is also ideal for meal-prep lunchboxes or feeding a crowd.

For the roasted squash

1 small butternut squash (approx. 600g/1lb 5oz)

2 red onions, chopped into chunks

4 garlic cloves, left whole

½ tsp chilli flakes

2 tbsp olive oil

2 x 200g/7oz blocks of extra-firm smoked (or regular) tofu, drained and chopped into cubes

50g/1¾oz/½ cup flaked/ sliced almonds

salt and pepper, to taste

For the sprout salad

180g/6¼oz/1 cup quinoa

260g/9¼oz/2 cups Brussels sprouts, shredded

100g/3½oz/4 cups cavolo nero (de-stemmed weight), shredded

4 spring onions/ scallions, thinly sliced

4 tbsp pomegranate seeds

2 sprigs of fresh mint, leaves only

For the dressing

4 tbsp extra virgin olive oil

2 tbsp lemon juice

a thumb-size piece of root ginger, peeled and grated

2 tbsp maple syrup

1. Preheat the oven to 200°C/400°F/Gas 6 and line a large baking sheet with baking parchment.

2. Scrub the squash, trim off the ends, cut in half and scoop out the seeds before slicing into small chunks or rounds. Add to the lined baking sheet with the red onions, garlic cloves, chilli flakes and olive oil. Season with salt and pepper and toss well. Bake in the oven for 15 minutes before adding the tofu cubes and flaked almonds. Toss again and bake for a further 15 minutes until the squash is tender and the tofu is golden.

3. Meanwhile, cook the quinoa for the salad according to the package directions, then leave to one side.

4. When the vegetables are done, remove the garlic cloves and squeeze out the garlic from the skins into a small bowl and mash with a fork.

5. For the dressing, add all the ingredients to the mashed garlic and whisk until smooth. Season with salt and pepper.

6. For the salad, add the shredded sprouts and kale to a large bowl with 2 tbsp of the dressing. Massage with your hands for 1 minute to soften the leaves. Now add in the roasted vegetables, cooked quinoa, spring onions and the rest of the dressing. Toss really well.

7. Divide the salad between four large plates and sprinkle over the pomegranate seeds and mint leaves. Enjoy straight away, or cool and refrigerate in a sealed container for 2–3 days, then serve cold.

Top Tip
Sweet potato would be delicious instead of butternut squash and you can also use pumpkin, if you prefer.

Lemony Asparagus Salad with Avocado Cream

Serves 4 | **Prep time:** 15 minutes | **Cook time:** 15 minutes

This salad is perfect for springtime when asparagus is at its peak and you're looking to switch up your quick and easy lunch meals. This one comes together in no time at all and contains a gorgeous array of vitamins, minerals and fibre, all of which protect and nourish your brain cells. The petit pois peas are great for adding protein, while the avocado cream tastes amazing and may help to reduce blood pressure and prevent cognitive decline.

For the roasted asparagus

2 bunches of asparagus, approx. 30 stalks in total, trimmed

1 tbsp olive oil

salt and pepper, to taste

For the salad

140g/5oz/1 cup spelt

4 handfuls of salad greens (e.g. rocket/arugula, lettuce and/or baby spinach)

140g/5oz/1 cup frozen petit pois, defrosted

4–5 radishes (120g/4¼oz/ 1 cup), cut into matchsticks

1 small cucumber, thinly sliced

2 spring onions/ scallions, thinly sliced

4 tbsp Homemade Pink Pickles (see page 31)

4 tbsp mixed seeds

a large sprig of fresh mint, leaves only

grated zest of 1 lemon

For the avocado cream

2 ripe avocados, peeled, pitted and roughly chopped

4 tbsp thick coconut yogurt, plus 2 tbsp extra if needed

2 tbsp runny smooth tahini

2 tbsp lemon juice

2 tsp white miso paste

1. Preheat the oven to 200°C/400°F/Gas 6 and line a large baking sheet with baking parchment.

2. Slice each asparagus stalk into three pieces and add to the lined baking sheet with the olive oil and some salt and pepper. Toss well to coat, then bake in the oven for 12–15 minutes, turning the baking sheet halfway through cooking. The asparagus will look crispy and tender when it's ready.

3. Meanwhile, cook the spelt according to the package directions, then drain and leave to one side.

4. For the avocado cream, add all the ingredients to a blender and blend until smooth and creamy, seasoning with salt and pepper. Stop to scrape down the sides as necessary and add 2 more tbsp of yogurt if needed to make it smoother.

5. To serve, divide the salad greens between four plates and top with the spelt, petit pois, radishes, cucumber and spring onions, then spoon over the avocado cream. Add the roasted asparagus on top, along with the pink pickles, mixed seeds, mint leaves and lemon zest.

6. Toss it all together, and enjoy. Eat straight away or refrigerate the salad in a sealed container for 2–3 days, ideally with the avocado cream stored separately – spoon this over and toss together just before serving.

Top Tip

You can use other whole grains rather than spelt here (which is not gluten-free). I like to use quinoa, buckwheat or giant couscous, too.

Smoky Red Pepper Pasta Salad

Serves 4 | **Prep time:** 15 minutes | **Cook time:** 10 minutes

Upgrade your lunchbox pasta salad with this nutrient-dense, high-protein and antioxidant-rich recipe. The roasted red pepper sauce is similar to a Romesco sauce with lots of Mediterranean flavours, with added creaminess from silken tofu. The hemp seeds are great for adding fatty acids to stimulate memory function, while the dark leafy kale is a powerhouse of vitamins, including vitamin B6, which is associated with brain function and cognition.

For the red pepper sauce

75g/2¾oz/½ cup roasted red peppers in oil (drained weight)

40g/1½oz/¼ cup sun-dried tomatoes (drained weight)

150g/5½oz silken tofu (drained weight)

40g/1½oz/¼ cup hulled hemp seeds

1 tbsp olive oil

1 tbsp nutritional yeast

1 tbsp lemon juice

1 garlic clove, peeled

1 tsp smoked paprika

salt and pepper, to taste

For the pasta

100g/3½oz/4 cups cavolo nero (de-stemmed weight)

2 tsp olive oil

a pinch of salt

1 x 400g/14oz can chickpeas/garbanzo beans, drained, rinsed and patted dry

320g/11¼oz/2 cups cherry tomatoes, halved

2 spring onions/ scallions, sliced

4 servings of whole-wheat pasta, cooked, drained and cooled

a few sprigs of fresh basil

4 tbsp Homemade Vegan Parmesan (see page 81)

1. For the red pepper sauce, add all the ingredients to a small blender and blend together until smooth, seasoning with salt and pepper.

2. For the pasta salad, finely chop the kale and add to a large mixing bowl with the olive oil and salt. Massage with your hands for 30 seconds to wilt the leaves (they will also darken).

3. Add the chickpeas to the kale, along with the cherry tomatoes, spring onions, cooked pasta and the red pepper sauce. Give it all a good toss to evenly coat the pasta with the sauce.

4. Divide the pasta salad between four bowls and serve with the basil sprigs and vegan parmesan.

5. Eat straight away, or refrigerate in a sealed container for 2–3 days and eat cold.

Top Tip

You can add other vegetables to this pasta salad, like chopped cucumber or diced (deseeded) red pepper instead of the tomatoes, and swap the chickpeas for canned butter/lima beans or lentils, too.

CHAPTER 3

dinner

Tandoori Tofu Traybake with Cucumber Raita

Serves 4 | **Prep time:** 15 minutes | **Cook time:** 30–40 minutes

Traybakes are perfect for a wholesome, filling and nutritious midweek meal for the family (or for leftovers the next day) and this Indian-spiced tofu traybake is a favourite. It is loaded with antioxidant-rich spices and herbs, protein-packed tofu and a vibrant array of vitamins and minerals from the veggies and kale, all of which help to boost our everyday brain function. The fermented coconut yogurt-based raita feeds our gut microbiome, which supports the gut-brain axis, which allows our bodies to thrive.

For the spice mix

2 tsp ground cumin

1 tsp hot smoked paprika

1 tsp ground ginger

½ tsp ground coriander

¼ tsp ground cardamom

For the roasted vegetables

2 red onions, cut into small chunks

2 red peppers, deseeded and cut into small chunks

2 large sweet potatoes, scrubbed and cut into small chunks (600g/1lb 5oz/4 heaped cups, once cut)

2 x 200g/7oz blocks of extra-firm tofu, drained and cut into small chunks

3 tbsp olive oil

salt and pepper, to taste

For the cucumber raita

1 cucumber (400g/14oz whole weight)

240g/8½oz/1 cup thick coconut yogurt

juice of 2 limes

1 tbsp chopped fresh mint

1 tbsp chopped fresh coriander/cilantro

a pinch of ground cumin

a pinch of hot smoked paprika or cayenne pepper

To serve

100g/3½oz/2 cups cavolo nero or kale (de-stemmed weight), shredded

4 tbsp pomegranate seeds

4 tbsp mixed seeds

1 ripe avocado, peeled, pitted and sliced or cubed (optional)

1. Preheat the oven to 180°C/350°F/Gas 4 and line two baking sheets with baking parchment.

2. Stir together all the ingredients for the spice mix.

3. For the roasted vegetables, add all the vegetables and the tofu to a large mixing bowl with the spice mix, the olive oil and some salt and pepper. Toss well, divide between the two lined baking sheets and spread out evenly.

4. Bake for 30–40 minutes, or until starting to crisp up and the potatoes are tender inside.

5. Meanwhile, using the same mixing bowl, add the shredded kale and a pinch of salt and massage with your hands for 1 minute to wilt the leaves.

6. To make the raita, grate the cucumber and place in a sieve or thin cloth and leave to sit over a bowl for 5 minutes. Squeeze out all the water (you can drink this cucumber water!) so you have about 160g/5¾oz/⅔ packed cup of grated cucumber.

7. Place the grated cucumber in a small bowl with the rest of the raita ingredients and stir well. Season with salt and pepper.

8. To serve, divide the kale between four plates, top with the roasted vegetables and tofu and spoon over the cucumber raita. Top with the pomegranate seeds, mixed seeds and avocado, if you like.

9. Enjoy straight away, or refrigerate leftovers separately in sealed containers for 2–3 days and eat cold. Or, to warm up leftovers, place them on a lined baking sheet (without the raita) and heat through in a preheated oven at 180°C/350°F/ Gas 4 for 10 minutes

Top Tip

You can swap around the vegetables in this recipe. For example, try courgette/zucchini or aubergine/eggplant instead of the red peppers.

Spiced Chickpea-stuffed Sweet Potatoes

Serves 4 | **Prep time:** 15 minutes | **Cook time:** 30 minutes

These sweet potatoes are spiced, saucy and packed with goodness. Sweet potatoes are a great source of antioxidants, vitamins and fibre to support digestive and brain health. They also contain beta-carotene, which your body converts to vitamin A to support the immune system. The chickpeas/garbanzo beans add protein and the tahini sauce is a delicious nut-free way to add in healthy fats and creaminess.

For the sweet potatoes

4 sweet potatoes

2 tbsp olive oil

salt and pepper, to taste

For the chickpeas

2 x 400g/14oz cans chickpeas/
garbanzo beans, drained
and rinsed (480g/1lb 1oz/
3 cups drained weight)

1 tsp hot smoked paprika

1 tsp ground cumin

½ tsp ground ginger

2 tsp maple syrup

2 tbsp tamari soy sauce

1 tbsp olive oil

For the tahini sauce

4 tbsp runny smooth tahini

a thumb-size piece of root
ginger, peeled and grated

1 small garlic clove, crushed

juice of 1 lime

1 tbsp tamari soy sauce

1 tbsp maple syrup

To finish and garnish

100g/3½oz/4 cups cavolo
nero or kale (de-stemmed
weight), shredded

2 spring onions/
scallions, sliced

4 tbsp pomegranate seeds

handful of fresh coriander/
cilantro or mint, chopped

2 tbsp sesame seeds

1. Preheat the oven to 200°C/400°F/Gas 6 and line two large baking sheets with baking parchment.

2. Scrub the sweet potatoes, then slice in half lengthways, rub with the olive oil and place, cut-side up, on one lined baking sheet. Season with salt and pepper.

3. For the chickpeas, pat the chickpeas dry with a dish towel. Add into a medium mixing bowl with the rest of the ingredients and some salt and pepper. Toss well, then spoon onto the second lined baking sheet (leaving any extra marinade in the bowl).

4. Place both baking sheets in the oven and bake for 25–30 minutes, tossing the chickpeas halfway through, until tender and crispy. The sweet potatoes will be tender inside.

5. Meanwhile, make the tahini sauce by stirring together all the ingredients until smooth. Slowly add water to reach a pourable consistency (about 2–3 tbsp).

6. Into the marinade bowl, add the cavolo nero or kale and massage well with your hands for 30 seconds to wilt the leaves.

7. To serve, place the sweet potatoes on plates and top with the kale and crispy chickpeas. Garnish with the spring onions, pomegranate seeds, herbs and sesame seeds and pour over the tahini sauce.

8. Enjoy straight away, or you can refrigerate the components separately in sealed containers for 2–3 days. Warm back up in the oven, as needed, or enjoy cold.

Top Tip

Any canned beans will work in place of chickpeas here, so feel free to try butter/lima beans, cannellini beans or even cooked Puy lentils.

Roasted Aubergine and Broccoli Lentil Curry

Serves 4 | **Prep time:** 15 minutes | **Cook time:** 20 minutes

Everyone loves a good curry and this one is loaded with brain-boosting ingredients like dark leafy spinach and broccoli, which are both great sources of fibre, B vitamins and vitamins C and K, plus they contain lots of antioxidants. Roasting the aubergine/eggplant in a sticky miso dressing makes it tender and delicious, while adding more plant diversity and polyphenols to feed the gut microbiome. This curry is creamy, warming and vibrant with fresh lime juice and garam masala spices and it's best served alongside some brown rice, flatbreads and fermented gut-healthy coconut yogurt.

For the roasted aubergine and broccoli

1 tbsp white or brown
   rice miso paste

1 tbsp tamari soy sauce

1 tbsp maple syrup

1 tbsp olive oil

½ tsp chilli flakes

1 aubergine/eggplant, cubed

1 head of broccoli,
   cut into florets

salt and pepper, to taste

For the curry

1 tbsp olive oil

1 red onion, finely chopped

4 garlic cloves, crushed

a thumb-size piece of root
   ginger, peeled and grated

2 tsp garam masala

1 tsp ground turmeric

½ tsp hot smoked paprika

1 x 400g/14oz can brown
   or green lentils, drained
   and rinsed (240g/8½oz/1½
   cups drained weight)

1 x 400ml/14fl oz can
   full-fat coconut milk

1 x 400g/14oz can
   chopped tomatoes

2 tbsp tomato purée/paste

1 tbsp white or brown
   rice miso paste

60g/2¼oz/2 cups baby
   spinach, chopped

juice of 1 lime

To serve

4 portions brown rice,
   cooked (and drained)

4 tbsp thick coconut yogurt

4 flatbreads of your choice

1 lime, cut into wedges

2 sprigs of fresh coriander/
   cilantro, leaves only

2 tbsp chopped roasted
   unsalted peanuts

1. Preheat the oven to 200°C/400°F/Gas 6 and line a large baking sheet with baking parchment.

2. For the roast veg, in a large mixing bowl, whisk together the miso paste, tamari, maple syrup, olive oil and chilli flakes with some salt and pepper. Add in the aubergine and broccoli and toss well. Pick out the aubergine pieces, place on the lined baking sheet and bake in the oven for 10 minutes. Remove from the oven, stir, then add the broccoli and bake for another 10 minutes until the aubergine is tender and sticky and the broccoli is starting to char.

3. Meanwhile, make the curry. Heat a large non-stick frying pan with the olive oil, and once hot, add the onion, garlic and ginger. Fry off over a high heat for 5 minutes to soften the onion, before adding in the ground spices with some salt and pepper. Fry for 1 minute, until smelling fragrant.

4. Now pour in the drained lentils, the coconut milk, chopped tomatoes, tomato purée and miso paste and stir well. Place a lid on the pan and cook over a medium heat for 10 minutes, stirring occasionally.

5. Once the sauce has simmered, add the spinach and lime juice and allow the leaves to wilt for 2–3 minutes.

6. Once the vegetables are roasted, stir half into the curry.

7. To plate up, add the cooked rice to four bowls and top with the curry. Swirl on the coconut yogurt and top with the remaining roasted vegetables. Serve with the flatbreads, lime wedges, coriander leaves and chopped peanuts.

8. Enjoy straight away, or allow the curry and vegetables to cool, then refrigerate in a sealed container all together for 2–3 days, or freeze for 1 month. Defrost (if frozen) and warm back up in a saucepan to eat.

Top Tips
Try courgette/zucchini instead of aubergine, or swap the broccoli for cauliflower. You can also leave out the peanuts to keep this recipe nut-free.

Creamy Roasted Butternut Squash and Spinach Dahl

Serves 4 as a main, serves 6 as a starter or small plate
Prep time: 15 minutes | **Cook time:** 35–40 minutes

I love this vegetable- and protein-packed dahl recipe and not only does it taste amazing, it is also loaded with antioxidants and other brain-boosting goodness. The range of spices, the vegetables and dark leafy spinach may aid your everyday brain function and memory, while the fermented miso paste and coconut yogurt feed your gut bacteria to strengthen the gut–brain axis and boost your overall wellbeing.

For the roasted squash

1 butternut squash, peeled, deseeded and cubed (600g/1lb 5oz/4 cups, once prepped)

1 tsp hot smoked paprika

1 tsp ground cumin

1½ tbsp olive oil

salt and pepper, to taste

For the dahl

1 tbsp olive oil

1 tsp ground cumin

½ tsp hot smoked paprika

½ tsp ground turmeric

½ tsp black mustard seeds

1 onion, cut into small dice

4 garlic cloves, crushed

a thumb-size piece of root ginger, peeled and grated

1 red pepper, deseeded and cut into small dice

200g/7oz/1 cup dried split red lentils

1 x 400g/14oz can chopped tomatoes

1 x 400ml/14fl oz can full-fat coconut milk

2 tbsp tomato purée/paste

2 tbsp runny smooth peanut butter

1 tbsp brown rice miso paste

juice of 1 lime

60g/2¼oz/2 cups baby spinach

To serve

4 tbsp thick coconut yogurt

cooked brown rice or other whole grain of your choice

pitta or naan breads

2 tbsp toasted sesame seeds

a handful of fresh coriander/cilantro or parsley

2 spring onions/ scallions, sliced

1. Start by preparing the roasted squash. Preheat the oven to 200°C/400°F/Gas 6 and line a large baking sheet with baking parchment.

2. Add the cubed squash and toss with the ground spices, olive oil and some salt and pepper. Bake in the oven for 25–30 minutes until tender and starting to char. Toss the cubes halfway through cooking so they cook evenly.

3. Meanwhile, prepare the dahl. Heat a large non-stick pan with the olive oil over a medium-high heat, and once hot, add the cumin, paprika, turmeric and mustard seeds. Fry off and pop for 1 minute before adding in the onion, garlic, ginger and red pepper. Stir well and fry for another 5 minutes to soften the onion.

4. Now add in the red lentils, tomatoes, coconut milk, 240ml/8½fl oz/1 cup water, tomato purée, peanut butter and miso paste. Season with salt and pepper to taste and stir well. Bring to a gentle bubble, then cover and cook over a medium heat for 25 minutes until really creamy. Stir often so the lentils don't stick to the bottom of the pan.

5. Before serving, add the lime juice and baby spinach to the pan and stir for 1–2 minutes to wilt the leaves. Stir in half of the roasted squash now.

6. To serve, spoon the dahl into bowls and top with some coconut yogurt and the rest of the roasted squash. Serve alongside some brown rice (or other grain) and pitta or naan breads, then I like to add some sesame seeds, fresh herbs and spring onions.

7. Eat straight away, or keep the dahl for later. Allow it to cool, then refrigerate in a sealed container for 3–5 days, or freeze for 1 month, then defrost (if frozen) and warm back up to eat.

Top Tips

You can add other vegetables to this dahl like aubergine/eggplant or courgette/zucchini instead of red pepper. Try swapping the spinach for kale, too.

Red Pepper Pesto Chickpea Traybake

Serves 4 | **Prep time:** 10 minutes | **Cook time:** 25 minutes

This traybake is a midweek winner with minimal prep. Walnuts help protect the brain against oxidative stress and inflammation, thanks to the high amounts of omega-3 fatty acids and antioxidants.

For the vegetables

1 white or red onion, cut into chunks

1 red pepper, deseeded and cut into chunks

1 courgette/zucchini, cut into ¼-moon slices

160g/5¾oz/1 cup cherry tomatoes, halved

1 x 400g/14oz can chickpeas/ garbanzo beans, drained, rinsed and patted dry (240g/ 8½oz/1½ cups drained weight)

2 garlic cloves, crushed

1 tbsp olive oil

½ tsp hot smoked paprika

½ tsp dried oregano

salt and pepper, to taste

For the red pepper pesto

100g/3½oz/2/3 cup roasted red peppers in oil (drained weight)

80g/2¾oz/½ cup sun-dried tomatoes (drained weight)

40g/1½oz/½ cup walnuts

2 tbsp nutritional yeast

2 tbsp extra virgin olive oil

1 tbsp lemon juice

1 garlic clove, crushed

For the bowls

180g/6¼oz/1 cup giant couscous or quinoa

75g/2¾oz/3 cups cavolo nero or kale, shredded

1 tsp olive oil

4 tbsp walnuts, crushed

4 tbsp pomegranate seeds

2 spring onions/scallions, sliced

1. Preheat the oven to 200°C/400°F/Gas 6 and line a large baking sheet with baking parchment.

2. Add the onion, red pepper, courgette, cherry tomatoes and chickpeas to the lined baking sheet. Now add the garlic, olive oil, paprika, oregano and some salt and pepper. Toss well, then roast in the oven for 20–25 minutes until the chickpeas are crispy and the vegetables are tender. Turn the baking sheet around halfway through.

3. Meanwhile, make the red pepper pesto by adding all the ingredients to a small food processor or blender and blitzing until smooth. Refrigerate in a sealed container for 3–5 days.

4. Cook the couscous or quinoa according to the package directions and leave to one side.

5. Add the kale to a medium bowl with 1 tsp of olive oil and a pinch of salt and massage with your hands for 30 seconds or so to wilt the leaves.

6. To serve, divide the couscous or quinoa between four bowls and add the kale. Top with the roasted vegetables and chickpeas and spoon over the red pepper pesto. Sprinkle over the walnuts, pomegranate seeds and spring onions, and enjoy.

7. Refrigerate leftovers in a sealed container for 2–3 days, then eat cold or warmed back up.

Top Tip

You can use any vegetables for this traybake – try swapping the courgette for aubergine/eggplant or cauliflower florets.

Green Goddess Pasta

Serves 4 | **Prep time:** 15 minutes | **Cook time:** 20 minutes

This pasta feels like a boost to your whole body with its vibrant, wholesome and creamy sauce and the array of vegetables it contains. The sauce is packed with dark leafy greens which are great for fuelling your brain, while providing calcium, iron and antioxidants, as well as high-protein silken tofu. Serve this green goddess sauce with your favourite whole-wheat pasta and some homemade vegan parmesan (see below), which is loaded with nuts and seeds, providing your body with valuable omega-3 fatty acids.

For the roasted vegetables

320g/11¼oz/2 cups cherry tomatoes, halved

1 large courgette/zucchini, cut into ¼-moon slices

½ tsp dried oregano

¼ tsp chilli flakes

1 tbsp olive oil

salt and pepper, to taste

For the homemade vegan parmesan

2 tbsp hulled hemp seeds

2 tbsp sunflower seeds or pine nuts

2 tbsp nutritional yeast

½ tsp garlic granules

½ tsp onion powder

For the green goddess sauce

1 tbsp olive oil

1 white onion, finely diced

3 garlic cloves, crushed

¼ red chilli, finely chopped (optional)

180g/6¼oz/3 cups baby spinach

30g/1oz/1 packed cup fresh basil leaves

1 x 300g/10½oz block of silken tofu, drained (290g/10¼oz drained weight)

1 tbsp lemon juice

2 tbsp nutritional yeast

2 tbsp hulled hemp seeds

To serve

4 servings of your favourite pasta (I like spelt or whole-wheat), cooked and drained, reserving 60ml/2fl oz/¼ cup pasta cooking water

a few sprigs of fresh basil (optional)

1. Preheat the oven to 200°C/400°F/Gas 6 and line a large baking sheet with baking parchment.

2. Add the tomatoes and courgette to the lined baking sheet and toss with the oregano, chilli flakes, olive oil and some salt and pepper. Roast in the oven for 20 minutes, until the tomatoes burst and are juicy. Turn the baking sheet around halfway through cooking.

3. Meanwhile, prepare the vegan parmesan by blitzing together all the ingredients in a blender or food processor, with salt and pepper to taste, to a fine crumbly mix. Tip into a jar or small bowl.

4. Make the green goddess sauce. Heat the olive oil in a large non-stick frying pan, and once hot, add the onion, garlic and chilli (if using). Fry off over a high heat for 5 minutes to soften before adding the baby spinach. Stir for 2–3 minutes until the spinach has wilted, is darker in colour and looks "wet". Transfer the mixture to the blender or food processor (no need to clean it out) with the rest of the sauce ingredients and season with salt and pepper. Blend until really smooth and creamy. Pour back into the frying pan and keep warm over a low heat.

5. To serve, add the cooked pasta to the pan with the green goddess sauce, add a splash of the reserved pasta cooking water and stir to warm through.

6. Divide the pasta between four bowls, topping with the roasted vegetables and sprinkling with some vegan parmesan. Add basil sprigs, if you like, and enjoy.

7. Leftover pasta is great cold for the next 2–3 days, kept refrigerated in a sealed container. Leftover vegan parmesan will keep in a sealed jar at room temperature for 1–2 weeks.

Top Tip

I like to use whole-wheat or spelt pasta to make this meal more wholesome, and if you're gluten-free, use your favourite gluten-free alternative – there are some great pulse- and legume-based ones.

Roasted Carrot and Chickpea Kale Bowls

Serves 4 | **Prep time:** 10 minutes | **Cook time:** 30 minutes

These bowls are vibrant, fresh and so delicious. They are well-balanced with wholegrain fibre, vegetables high in antioxidants, protein-rich chickpeas/garbanzo beans and kale, which is great for helping our brain function. The creamy sauce is ready in less than a minute but is next-level with tons of flavour and creaminess. I guarantee you'll be spooning it over everything.

For the roasted vegetables

4 large carrots (or 16 baby carrots), washed

1 x 400g/14oz can chickpeas/garbanzo beans, drained, rinsed and patted dry (240g/8½oz/1½ cups drained weight)

1 tsp ground cumin

1 tsp hot smoked paprika

1 tbsp olive oil

salt and pepper, to taste

For the sauce

1 x 300g/10½oz block of silken tofu, drained (290g/10¼oz drained weight)

2 tbsp runny smooth tahini

2 tbsp nutritional yeast

1 tbsp lemon juice

1 tbsp apple cider vinegar

1 tbsp chopped fresh mint

1 tbsp chopped fresh parsley

For the salad

180g/6¼oz/1 cup quinoa

100g/3½oz/4 cups cavolo nero or kale (de-stemmed weight), shredded

1 tsp olive oil

a pinch of salt

4 handfuls of rocket/arugula

8 radishes, thinly sliced

1 ripe avocado, cubed

4 tbsp sauerkraut

4 tbsp sunflower seeds

1. Start by preparing the roasted vegetables. Preheat the oven to 180°C/350°F/Gas 4 and line a large baking sheet with baking parchment.

2. Trim the tops from the carrots, slice into small chunks and add to the lined baking sheet.

3. Add the chickpeas to the carrots with both spices, the olive oil and some salt and pepper and toss well. Roast in the oven for 30 minutes until tender and turning crispy. Stir the mixture halfway through.

4. Meanwhile, make the sauce. Add the tofu, tahini, nutritional yeast, lemon juice and vinegar to a small blender with some salt and pepper and blend until really creamy. Now stir in the chopped herbs, then refrigerate in a sealed container (until needed) for 3–5 days.

5. Cook the quinoa for the salad according to the package directions, then leave to one side.

6. Add the kale to a large bowl with the olive oil and salt and massage with your hands for 30 seconds to wilt the leaves.

7. When ready to serve, divide the kale between the bowls and top with the quinoa, some rocket and the roasted carrots and chickpeas, then add the radishes, avocado and sauerkraut. Spoon or pour over the sauce and top with the sunflower seeds.

8. Enjoy straight away, or refrigerate in sealed containers for 2–3 days (it's best to add the rocket on the same day as eating the salad, otherwise the leaves will wilt).

Top Tips

You can use buckwheat or couscous instead of quinoa for the salad, if preferred. Try swapping the carrots for cubed sweet potato, too.

Sesame-crusted Tofu Noodle Salad
with Peanut Satay Sauce

Serves 4 | **Prep time:** 20 minutes + 20 minutes (or 1–2 hours) marinating | **Cook time:** 20 minutes

Fast, fresh and vibrant, these noodle bowls are a big favourite of mine. The protein-rich tofu is tender inside, packed with flavour and has an easy-to-create but tasty crunchy golden sesame crust. It pairs so well with a drizzle of creamy peanut satay sauce, and all the vegetables add a range of vitamin goodness to support your brain.

Top Tip
You can use any vegetables you like here, such as fennel, courgette/zucchini, broccoli, white cabbage or kale.

For the tofu

2 x 200g/7oz blocks of extra-firm tofu, drained

2 tbsp tamari soy sauce

1 tbsp sesame oil

1 tbsp lime juice

1 tbsp maple syrup

1 garlic clove, crushed

a thumb-size piece of root ginger, peeled and grated

salt and pepper, to taste

For the satay sauce

leftover marinade (from above)

3 tbsp smooth peanut butter

1–2 tbsp full-fat coconut milk

For the tofu coating

35g/1¼oz/¼ cup any plain/all-purpose flour of your choice

80ml/2¾fl oz/1/3 cup plant-based milk

3 tbsp mixed white and black sesame seeds

1 tbsp nutritional yeast

olive oil, for brushing/spraying

For the noodle bowls

4 nests of dried noodles of your choice

1 red pepper, thinly sliced

1 large carrot (approx. 160g/5¾oz), sliced

½ cucumber (approx. 200g/7oz), halved and thinly sliced

100g/3½oz/1 cup red cabbage, shredded

1 red chilli, sliced (optional)

1 spring onion/scallion, sliced

2 tbsp chopped fresh mint and/or coriander/cilantro

45g/1½oz/1/3 cup roasted peanuts, chopped

1. Start by preparing the tofu and the marinade. Drain away any excess liquid from the tofu. Cut each block in half widthways, then slice each half into 3 equal rectangles, so you have 12 in total. In a small bowl, whisk together all the other tofu ingredients to make the marinade. Now dip each piece of tofu in the marinade to coat and place on a plate so they are all touching. Leave for 20 minutes, or preferably if you have time, cover and refrigerate for 1–2 hours.

2. Make the sauce. To the leftover marinade above, add the peanut butter and coconut milk. Whisk until smooth and leave to one side.

3. In one shallow bowl, whisk together the flour and milk for the coating and season with salt and pepper. In a second shallow bowl, mix the sesame seeds and nutritional yeast.

4. Preheat the oven to 180°C/350°F/Gas 4 and line one or two baking sheets with baking parchment.

5. To make the crusted tofu, take one piece of tofu at a time, and dip it into the flour mix to coat all over and then dip it straight into the sesame seed mix. Flip over to ensure all the tofu is coated, then place on a lined baking sheet. Repeat with all 12 pieces. Brush or spray with olive oil.

6. Bake in the oven for 10 minutes, then remove from the oven and use a spatula to carefully flip over each piece of tofu. Brush/spray this top side with more oil and then bake again for 10 minutes until golden and crispy.

7. Meanwhile, cook the noodles according to the package directions, then rinse well with cold water to stop further cooking.

8. Prepare all the vegetables as indicated – you want them all roughly the same size (except the chilli and spring onion).

9. Toss the noodles with all the sliced vegetables (reserving the chilli and spring onion) and half the satay sauce. Divide them between four bowls and top each portion with three pieces of tofu, the chilli, if using, the spring onion, herbs and peanuts. Drizzle over the remaining sauce, and enjoy.

10. Refrigerate leftovers in a sealed container for 2–3 days and eat cold. Or, to eat warm, heat back up in a large non-stick frying pan over a medium-high heat until warmed through.

Mediterranean Nourish Bowls

Serves 4 | **Prep time:** 15 minutes | **Cook time:** 30 minutes

These Mediterranean nourish bowls are full of flavour, colour and texture and make for a quick and easy midweek dinner. The range of vibrant vegetables, including sweet and new potatoes, and the beans will add so much diversity to your plate, which in turn feeds your brain in different ways. The omega-3 fatty acids in the creamy tahini dressing are great for memory function, while the leafy greens are known for their antioxidant properties, important for overall wellbeing.

For the roasted vegetables

600g/1lb 5oz/5 cups potatoes (half sweet potatoes, scrubbed, and half baby new potatoes), finely chopped

2 red peppers, deseeded and cut into small chunks

1 tsp dried mixed herbs

a pinch of chilli flakes

2 tbsp olive oil

320g/11¼oz/2 cups cherry or baby plum tomatoes, halved

salt and pepper, to taste

For the beans

1 x 400g/14oz can cannellini beans, drained and rinsed (240g/8½oz/1½ cups drained weight)

80g/2¾oz/½ cup pitted green or black olives, sliced

120g/4¼oz artichokes in oil (drained weight), chopped

4 tbsp chopped fresh mixed herbs (e.g. chives, basil and mint)

juice of 1 lemon

For the tahini dressing

4 tbsp runny smooth tahini

2 tbsp extra virgin olive oil

1 tsp brown rice miso paste

juice of 1 lemon

2–3 tbsp water

To serve

4 large handfuls of mixed salad leaves (e.g. lettuce, baby spinach and rocket/arugula)

1 quantity of Tofu Feta (see page 32) (optional)

4 tbsp mixed seeds

1. Preheat the oven to 180°C/350°F/Gas 4 and line a large baking sheet with baking parchment.

2. Place the potatoes and red peppers on the lined baking sheet, ensuring they don't overlap too much (use two baking sheets, if needed). Toss with the dried herbs, chilli flakes, olive oil and some salt and pepper. Roast in the oven for 10 minutes, then add the tomatoes, toss around gently and roast for another 20 minutes. The potatoes will be soft inside and starting to crisp on the outside.

3. Meanwhile, prepare the beans. In a large bowl, toss together the beans, olives, artichokes, herbs and lemon juice with some salt and pepper.

4. For the tahini dressing, stir together all the ingredients in a small bowl until smooth, adding enough of the water to reach a pourable consistency. Season with salt and pepper.

5. When ready to serve, divide the salad leaves between four plates. Top with the roasted vegetables and the herby beans, then pour over the dressing. Sprinkle some tofu feta on top, if you like, and some mixed seeds, and enjoy.

6. To keep the salad for later, keep the salad leaves separately and add these just before serving. Refrigerate the cooled roasted vegetables and the tahini dressing in separate sealed containers for 2–3 days. Toss it all together before serving cold.

Top Tip

This is great for lunchboxes the next day – simply store the salad leaves on top of the roasted vegetables, herby beans and dressing to keep them fresh and then toss together to eat.

Creamy Arrabbiata Beans

Serves 4 generously | **Prep time:** 10 minutes | **Cook time:** 30 minutes

These creamy, warming beans are flavoured with fresh chilli for a little kick as well as packing in lots of brain-friendly foods like dark leafy spinach and coconut yogurt. These are a family favourite and are delicious mopped up with bread or served with your favourite whole grain or pasta.

For the beans

2 x 400g/14oz cans cannellini beans (480g/1lb 1oz/3 cups drained weight)

1 tbsp olive oil

1 white onion, finely diced

3 large garlic cloves, crushed

1 red chilli (or less, to your taste), finely diced

a pinch of salt

420g/15oz/4 cups cherry tomatoes, halved

½ tsp dried oregano

120g/4¼oz/4 cups baby spinach

2 tbsp chopped fresh basil, plus extra to serve

For the sauce

2 tbsp tomato purée/paste

1 tbsp brown rice miso paste

60g/2¼oz/¼ cup thick coconut yogurt

40g/1½oz/¼ cup sun-dried tomatoes (drained weight)

2 tbsp nutritional yeast (optional)

salt and pepper, to taste

To serve

4 tbsp thick coconut yogurt

chopped nuts/seeds e.g. Dukkah (see page 54) or Homemade Vegan Parmesan (see page 81)

your favourite bread or cooked whole grain

1. Divide up the beans first: drain both cans of beans (reserving the beans and liquid separately) and keep 360g/12¾oz/2¼ cups for the saucepan, and 120g/4¼oz/¾ cup for the sauce. You will have about 300ml/10½fl oz/1¼ cups of liquid from the cans; keep this to one side.

2. Heat the olive oil in a large non-stick pan over a high heat until hot, then add the onion, garlic and chilli and fry off with the pinch of salt for 5 minutes until softened. Now add in the tomatoes and oregano and cook over a high heat with a lid on for 10 minutes until the tomatoes burst.

3. Meanwhile, make the sauce. In a small blender, add 120g/4¼oz/¾ cup of the beans with 60ml/2fl oz/¼ cup of their liquid with the rest of the sauce ingredients and some salt and pepper. Blend until creamy.

4. Now add the sauce and the rest of the beans into the tomato mixture, plus 120ml/4fl oz/½ cup of the bean liquid, to start. Season with some black pepper and stir well. Allow to bubble for 10 minutes, with a lid on, stirring occasionally, until warmed through. Add more liquid (60ml/2fl oz/¼ cup, plus more) if needed.

5. Add the spinach and basil to the pan and stir to allow the spinach to wilt.

6. Ladle the warmed beans into bowls, spoon swirls of coconut yogurt on top, then finish with some extra basil, black pepper and the chopped nuts/seeds. Serve with your favourite bread or whole grain.

7. Refrigerate any leftover cooled beans in a sealed container for 2–3 days, or freeze for 1 month, then defrost (if frozen) and warm back up to enjoy.

CHAPTER 4

snacks & dessert

Homemade Dark Chocolate Bars Three Ways

Makes 2 large bars or 20 smaller bars
Prep time: 20 minutes + 1 hour chilling | **Cook time:** 5 minutes

Dark/bittersweet chocolate is a superfood in itself, thanks to the flavonoids and polyphenols it contains. Flavonoids are important for helping our brains learn and create memories, while polyphenols can help to lower blood pressure and improve brain health. This homemade chocolate also contains antioxidants which promote better brain health, plus it melts in the mouth and is so delicious. It makes gorgeous gifts and you can add in anything you like!

For the chocolate recipe

120g/4¼oz/1 cup cacao butter buttons, finely chopped

2 tbsp maple syrup

1 tbsp runny smooth cashew or almond butter

25g/1oz/¼ cup raw cacao powder

a pinch of salt

For the fruit and nut bars

90g/3¼oz/¾ cup mixed dried fruits and raw nuts of your choice, chopped

For the crispy bars

20g/¾oz/¾ cup puffed rice cereal

1. To prepare the chocolate, add the cacao butter to a heatproof bowl, then either melt in the microwave on High for about 2 minutes, stirring every 15 seconds or so, or melt over a pan of simmering water (known as a bain-marie), until just melted. It will become a golden clear liquid.

2. Add in the maple syrup and cashew or almond butter and whisk until smooth.

3. Sift in the cacao powder and add the salt, then whisk until glossy and no lumps of cacao powder remain.

4. If making plain chocolate, pour the chocolate into the silicone moulds now (see Top Tip), then carefully transfer to the refrigerator to set.

5. If making one of the other two flavoured bars, either add the dried fruit and nut mix or the puffed rice cereal and stir to combine. Pour into the silicone moulds, then chill in the refrigerator to set.

6. Thinner chocolate moulds will take 1 hour to set, thicker truffle-style shapes may take longer.

7. Once set, carefully press the chocolate bars out of the moulds.

8. Enjoy straight away, or keep in a sealed container at room temperature for 1 week.

Top Tip

It is easiest to use silicone moulds for these chocolate bars (I use either two 8 x 16cm/3½ x 6½ in moulds or 20 smaller moulds, each about 2.5 x 5cm/1 x 2in). Place the moulds on a chopping board before pouring in the chocolate, so you can pick them up easily.

Homemade DARK CHOCOLATE

Top Tip
You can play around with the flavours in this superfood loaf. Try adding a pinch of chilli flakes, or ½ tsp of hot smoked paprika or ground cumin for a smoky bread.

Superfood Buckwheat and Seed Bread

Makes 1 loaf (10–12 slices) | **Prep time:** 20 minutes + cooling | **Cook time:** 40 minutes

Upgrade your toast and sandwiches with this nourishing, hearty, brain-boosting superfood loaf. It is naturally gluten-free and contains lots of omega-3 healthy fats and antioxidants, which help to support good brain function. This recipe requires no yeast or kneading, either. I love to toast a slice and top it with avocado and fresh herbs.

For the loaf

4 tbsp chia seeds or ground flaxseed (I like half of each)

240ml/8½fl oz/1 cup lukewarm water

300g/10½oz/1½ cups buckwheat flour

3 tsp baking powder

2 tbsp nutritional yeast

2 tsp dried mixed herbs

1 tsp garlic granules

1 tsp salt

40g/1½oz/¼ cup sunflower seeds

2 tbsp hulled hemp seeds

160ml/5¼fl oz/⅔ cup lukewarm water

4 tbsp extra virgin olive oil

2 tbsp thick coconut yogurt

black pepper, to taste

To finish

1 tbsp mixed seeds (e.g. hemp, sunflower and chia seeds)

1. Preheat the oven to 180°C/350°F/Gas 4 and line a 23 x 13cm/9 x 5in loaf pan with baking parchment.

2. Into a large mixing bowl, add the chia seeds or ground flaxseed and the warm water. Whisk well, then leave for 10 minutes to thicken and form a gel.

3. Now, into the same bowl, add all the other ingredients for the loaf, seasoning with black pepper as desired. Stir really well to a thick and gloopy batter.

4. Pour the batter into the lined loaf pan and press down to fill in all the gaps. Smooth over the top and use a knife to gently make a score down the middle.

5. To finish the loaf, sprinkle the top with any seeds you like.

6. Bake in the oven for 40 minutes until well-risen, golden brown on top and an inserted skewer comes out clean.

7. Leave the bread to rest in the loaf pan for 10 minutes on a wire/cooling rack before carefully lifting the loaf out and cooling it fully on the rack.

8. Once cool, use a sharp knife to cut the loaf into slices and eat straight away.

9. Keep the bread fresh, wrapped well, in the refrigerator for 3–5 days, or freeze for 1–2 months. I like to slice the whole loaf, then keep it in the freezer to take out (and defrost) slices as and when I like.

Dark Chocolate Avocado Pistachio Truffles

Makes 20 | **Prep time:** 20 minutes + 40–50 minutes chilling

Dark/bittersweet chocolate truffles are the most indulgent and delicious after-dinner dessert and these are bursting with good-for-you ingredients. They melt in your mouth and no one will be able to tell that they are loaded with vitamins, minerals and monounsaturated fats from the avocado. This is great news for the brain and promoting healthy blood flow. They also contain cocoa powder which is a natural stimulant and shown to improve memory and mood.

For the truffles

- 170g/6oz dark/bittersweet chocolate, finely chopped
- 1 ripe avocado, peeled, pitted and mashed (150g/5½oz/⅔ cup once mashed)
- 2 tbsp runny smooth peanut butter
- 4 tbsp coconut cream or thick coconut yogurt
- 4 tbsp unsweetened cocoa powder or raw cacao powder
- 2 tbsp maple syrup
- a pinch of salt

For the chocolate coating

- 85g/3oz dark/bittersweet chocolate, finely chopped
- 2 tsp coconut oil
- 2 tbsp crushed pistachios

1. For the truffles, put the dark chocolate into a heatproof bowl and warm through until melted (either in the microwave on High in 15-second bursts, or over a pan of simmering water, known as a bain-marie). Allow to cool down slightly while you move on.

2. Place the mashed avocado in a food processor or blender with the peanut butter, coconut cream or yogurt, cocoa/cacao powder, maple syrup and salt. Blend until really smooth and no lumps remain.

3. Now pour the melted chocolate into the food processor/blender and blend again until thick and combined, stopping to scrape down the sides as necessary. Transfer the mixture to the refrigerator for 10 minutes to firm up.

4. Line a large tray or plate with baking parchment.

5. Using a spoon, divide the truffle mix into 20 even portions and then roll into golf ball-size balls, placing them on the lined tray/plate. Return to the refrigerator for 30 minutes.

6. Meanwhile, melt together the dark chocolate and coconut oil for the coating (as above), until smooth and combined.

7. Once firm, dip each truffle into the chocolate coating to evenly coat all over, and allow excess chocolate to drip off. Return the dipped truffles to the baking parchment and sprinkle the tops with the crushed pistachios while the chocolate is still wet.

8. The chocolate truffles will set quickly, but if they are still wet, return to the refrigerator for 10 minutes. Enjoy straight away, or refrigerate in a sealed container for 3–5 days.

Top Tip
Make these truffles nut-free by using sunflower seed butter or runny smooth tahini instead of peanut butter and swapping the pistachios for desiccated coconut.

Snickers-style Protein Bars

Makes 10 | **Prep time:** 20 minutes + 2–4 hours chilling

These tempting homemade protein bars are my vegan take on the popular chocolate-covered peanutty caramel bars. They are made with wholesome high-protein and high-fibre ingredients, are naturally sweetened with dates and packed with healthy fats. The flavonoids in the dark chocolate aid learning and memory formation.

Top Tip
Roast your own peanuts by adding all the nuts to a baking sheet and roasting in a preheated oven at 180°C/350°F/Gas 4 for 10 minutes until smelling fragrant. Allow to cool fully before making these bars.

For the base

100g/3½oz/1 cup rolled oats

70g/2½oz/½ cup
    roasted peanuts

25g/1oz/¼ cup vegan
    protein powder
    (or more oats)

a pinch of salt

60g/2¼oz/¼ cup runny
    smooth peanut butter

2 tbsp maple syrup

1 tbsp coconut oil, melted

1 tbsp plant-based milk

For the filling

4 Medjool dates, pitted
    (approx. 80g/2¾oz/½
    cup once pitted)

60ml/2fl oz/¼ cup
    plant-based milk

80g/2¾oz/1/3 cup runny
    smooth peanut butter

2 tbsp coconut oil, melted

1 tsp vanilla extract

a pinch of salt

70g/2½oz/½ cup
    roasted peanuts

For the chocolate coating

112g/4oz dark/
    bittersweet chocolate,
    chopped or in chips

1 tsp coconut oil

extra roasted peanuts,
    crushed

flaky salt (optional)

1. Line a 15cm/6in square baking pan with baking parchment. Soak the dates for the filling in boiling water for 10 minutes and then drain.

2. First, make the base. Add the oats and peanuts to a small blender and blitz to a fine flour-like texture. Add this to a small mixing bowl with the rest of the ingredients for the base. Stir to a sticky mixture that holds together when pressed between two fingers.

3. Pour all the base mixture into the lined baking pan and press down firmly to make a compact layer. Chill in the refrigerator while you continue.

4. To make the filling, add the soaked and drained dates, the milk, peanut butter, coconut oil, vanilla and salt to the blender (no need to clean it out) and blend until really smooth. Stop once or twice to scrape down the sides as necessary.

5. Remove the baking pan from the refrigerator and spread the caramel filling all over the base. Sprinkle over the peanuts and press down lightly. Return the pan to the refrigerator (or freezer) for 2–4 hours, or until firm to touch.

6. For the chocolate coating, melt together the chocolate and coconut oil in a heatproof bowl over a pan of simmering water (known as a bain-marie) or in the microwave on High in 15-second bursts until glossy.

7. When ready to coat, lift the bar mixture out of the baking pan and use a sharp, warmed knife to slice it into 10 even pieces. Now dip each one into the melted chocolate, top down, to coat the peanut and caramel middle (but not the bottom). Allow the excess to drip off and then transfer to a plate, chocolate-up.

8. While the chocolate is still warm, sprinkle over some crushed peanuts, then a little flaky salt, if desired. Leave to set in the refrigerator for 10 minutes.

9. Enjoy straight away, or refrigerate these bars in a sealed container for 1 week, or freeze for 1 month, then defrost before eating.

Edible Brownie Cookie Dough Jars

Makes 4 small jars | Prep time: 15 minutes

There is nothing quite like eating raw cookie dough or brownie batter straight from the bowl, so this healthier and delicious no-bake dessert combines both of these together. The star of the show is the hidden chickpeas/garbanzo beans, which make for a nutrient-dense dough that's sticky, fibrous and naturally high in protein. The polyphenols and flavonoids in the dark chocolate can support cognition and promote better brain health as you age, while the oat flour will keep you satiated for longer thanks to the fibre content. I've also included the option to make these into brownie or cookie dough balls, which are great for fuelling your brain on the go.

For the main mix

1 x 400g/14oz can chickpeas/garbanzo beans, drained and rinsed (240g/8½oz/1½ cups drained weight)

60g/2¼oz/¼ cup runny smooth peanut butter

60g/2¼oz/¼ cup maple syrup

2 tbsp plant-based milk

1 tbsp vanilla extract

a pinch of salt

For the add-ins

4 tbsp oat flour or almond flour

85g/3oz/½ cup dark/bittersweet chocolate chips

2 tbsp unsweetened cocoa powder or raw cacao powder

To serve (optional)

4 tbsp runny smooth peanut butter

flaky salt

1. Add the chickpeas to a small blender or food processor along with the peanut butter, maple syrup, milk, vanilla and salt and blend together until really smooth. Stop to scrape down the sides as necessary.

2. Divide the mixture equally between two bowls.

3. For the cookie dough, stir the oat or almond flour into one bowlful until sticky, then fold in half the chocolate chips until combined.

4. For the brownie batter, sift the cocoa or cacao powder into the second bowlful and stir until combined, before folding in the rest of the chocolate chips.

5. To serve, layer up small jars with spoonfuls of the cookie dough and brownie batter, then drizzle over the peanut butter and sprinkle with flaky salt, if you like.

6. Enjoy straight away, or cover tightly and refrigerate for 2–3 days.

Top Tip

You can also scoop the cookie dough and brownie batter mixes, from steps 3 and 4, into balls, then place on a baking sheet lined with baking parchment and freeze for 1 hour to enjoy as snack balls. Refrigerate in a sealed container for 2–3 days.

Black Forest Lava Cakes

Serves 4 | **Prep time:** 20 minutes + 10 minutes cooling | **Cook time:** 21 minutes

Dark/bittersweet chocolate, cherries and coconut "cream" come together perfectly in these nourishing plant-based lava cakes. They have a gooey, chocolatey melting middle and are packed with flavonoid-rich cocoa to support brain health, espresso coffee and peanut butter. The polyphenols in coffee promote memory, learning and cognitive function, while cherries are high in antioxidants, which aid the brain's plasticity by improving connections between brain cells and fighting free radicals.

Top Tips

Patience is key for this recipe; ensure you allow them to rest for 10 minutes before inverting onto plates, as they are delicate straight from the oven.
Also, feel free to swap the cherries for blueberries or raspberries.

For the lava cakes

80g/2¾oz/heaped ½
  cup (pitted weight)
  fresh cherries, pitted
  and finely chopped

100g/3½oz/1 cup +
  1 tbsp oat flour

4 tbsp Homemade
  "Nutella" (see page 134),
  or 8 squares of dark/
  bittersweet chocolate

85g/3oz/½ cup dark/
  bittersweet chocolate chips

120g/4¼oz/½ cup runny
  smooth peanut butter

120ml/4fl oz/½ cup
  maple syrup

60ml/2fl oz/¼ cup
  plant-based milk

60ml/2fl oz/¼ cup warm
  brewed espresso coffee

60ml/2fl oz/¼ cup olive oil

60g/2¼oz/¼ cup thick
  coconut yogurt

50g/1¾oz/½ cup
  unsweetened
  cocoa powder

½ tsp baking powder

a pinch of salt

To serve

4 tbsp dark/bittersweet
  chocolate chips

4 scoops of thick coconut
  yogurt or dairy-
  free ice cream

4 fresh cherries
  with stalks on

1 tbsp unsweetened
  cocoa powder

1. Toss the chopped cherries with the 1 tbsp of oat flour in a small bowl. Scoop the "Nutella" into four balls onto a plate, then refrigerate until set while you make the cakes.

2. Preheat the oven to 180°C/350°F/Gas 4 and grease the sides and base of four 10cm/4in ramekins. Line the base of each with baking parchment.

3. Add the chocolate chips and peanut butter to a large heatproof bowl and warm in the microwave on High in 15-second bursts (or over a pan of simmering water, known as a bain-marie) until melted and smooth, stirring occasionally. Leave to cool for 5 minutes.

4. Whisk in the maple syrup, milk, espresso, olive oil and coconut yogurt until smooth and glossy.

5. Pour in the remaining oat flour and sift in the cocoa powder and baking powder. Add the salt and whisk to a smooth, thick batter. Fold in the chopped cherries until combined.

6. Fill each ramekin half-full with the chocolate cake batter and then press a ball of chilled "nutella" (or 2 squares of dark chocolate) into the middle of each. Top with the rest of the cake batter, covering the "nutella" ball/chocolate. Smooth over the tops.

7. Bake in the oven for about 21 minutes, or until firm to touch and the tops are starting to crisp at the sides and no longer look wet and shiny.

8. Cool the cakes in the ramekins for 10 minutes (see Top Tips), then carefully run a palette knife/metal spatula or spatula around the edges to loosen them.

9. Place a small plate on top of each ramekin and carefully flip over to invert onto the plate. Sprinkle over the chocolate chips and they'll start to melt.

10. Top each with a scoop of yogurt or ice cream and a cherry, then dust over the cocoa powder before enjoying straight away.

11. Allow leftover cakes to cool in the ramekins, or on plates, then refrigerate in a sealed container for 2–3 days. Warm back up in a preheated oven at 180°C/350°F/Gas 4 for 5 minutes, or better still, heat up (one at a time) in the microwave on High for 30–60 seconds.

Sun-dried Tomato and Olive Muffins

Makes 12 | **Prep time:** 15 minutes + cooling | **Cook time:** 20 minutes

These savoury muffins are a powerhouse of nutrition and are delicious to snack on all day long. They are packed with Mediterranean flavours from the olives and sun-dried tomatoes, while the baby spinach is an excellent source of fibre and minerals like iron. They are super fluffy and moreish and are loaded with healthy omega fatty acids from the mixed seeds, which our brains love, as they may help to reduce memory loss and support daily brain function.

For the muffins

360ml/12fl oz/1⅓ cups plant-based milk

2 tsp apple cider vinegar

3 tbsp olive oil

280g/10oz/2 cups plain/all-purpose flour or gluten-free* plain/all-purpose flour

70g/2½oz/½ cup wholemeal/whole-wheat spelt flour or buckwheat flour*

4 tbsp nutritional yeast

½ tsp hot smoked paprika

2 tsp baking powder

½ tsp bicarbonate of soda/baking soda

60g/2¼oz/½ cup pitted olives, sliced

60g/2¼oz/½ cup sun-dried tomatoes from a jar (drained weight), finely chopped

60g/2¼oz/2 cups baby spinach, chopped

4 tbsp mixed seeds

salt and pepper, to taste

1. Preheat the oven to 180°C/350°F/Gas 4 and line a 12-hole muffin pan with paper muffin cases/liners.

2. In a large mixing bowl, whisk together the milk and vinegar and leave to one side for 5 minutes to curdle. Now whisk in the olive oil until smooth.

3. Into the mix, sift the flours, then add the nutritional yeast, paprika, baking powder and bicarbonate of soda and season with salt and pepper. Whisk to a smooth, thick, lump-free batter.

4. Fold in the olives, sun-dried tomatoes and spinach until they are evenly mixed in.

5. Scoop the batter evenly into the muffin cases, filling to the tops, then sprinkle over the mixed seeds.

6. Bake in the oven for 20–22 minutes, until golden on top, well-risen and an inserted skewer comes out clean.

7. Allow the muffins to cool in the pan for 5 minutes, then carefully remove and cool fully on a wire/cooling rack.

8. Enjoy the muffins cold, and refrigerate any leftovers in a sealed container for 3–5 days. You can also freeze the muffins for 1 month, then defrost before eating.

Top Tips

*If using gluten-free flour, add ½ tsp of xanthan gum to your flour blend if it doesn't already contain it, and use gluten-free baking powder. Also swap the spelt flour for buckwheat flour. These muffins are delicious alongside Hidden-Vegetable Squash and Tomato Soup (see page 144).

Hidden Vegetable Chocolate Fudge Cake

Serves 10 | **Prep time:** 25 minutes + cooling | **Cook time:** 47 minutes

You will never be able to tell that this rich and fudgy chocolate cake contains a green vegetable (grated courgette/zucchini) and also avocado in the frosting. They boost the nutrition of this cake by adding vitamins and minerals, while the mashed banana naturally sweetens the batter and the coconut yogurt is great for the gut. It also contains cocoa powder, a natural stimulant for the brain, so this really is a super-food bake for all the family to enjoy.

For the chocolate cake

1 medium courgette/ zucchini, grated

180ml/6¼fl oz/¾ cup plant-based milk

½ tbsp apple cider vinegar

105g/3¾oz/¾ cup coconut sugar

80g/2¾oz/1/3 cup mashed banana or unsweetened shop-bought apple sauce

60ml/2fl oz/¼ cup olive oil

1 tbsp ground flaxseed

1 tsp vanilla extract

175g/6oz/1¼ cups plain/ all-purpose flour or gluten-free* plain/ all-purpose flour

38g/1¼oz/3⁄8 cup unsweetened cocoa powder

1¼ tsp baking powder

¼ tsp bicarbonate of soda/baking soda

a pinch of salt

85g/3oz dark/bittersweet chocolate chips

For the frosting

1 ripe avocado, halved, pitted and peeled (you need 180g/6¼oz of flesh)

80ml/2¾fl oz/1/3 cup maple syrup

25g/1oz/¼ cup unsweetened cocoa powder

2 tbsp thick coconut yogurt

1 tsp vanilla extract

a pinch of salt

To decorate

a handful of fresh berries (e.g. strawberries, blueberries) or pomegranate seeds

1 tbsp chopped dark/ bittersweet chocolate

1. Preheat the oven to 180°C/350°F/Gas 4. Grease and line a 20cm/8in round cake pan (medium-depth) with baking parchment.

2. Place the grated courgette in a piece of muslin cloth/ cheesecloth to drain. Leave for 10 minutes, then squeeze out all the excess water (you'll start with approx. 160g/5¾oz of courgette and be left with 100g/3½oz).

3. Meanwhile, in a large mixing bowl, whisk together the milk and vinegar, then leave to curdle for 5 minutes. Add in the coconut sugar, mashed banana or apple sauce, olive oil, ground flaxseed and vanilla and whisk to combine.

4. Sift in the flour, cocoa powder, baking powder and bicarbonate of soda and add the salt. Whisk to a smooth, thick batter. Fold in the chocolate chips and the squeezed-out grated courgette (breaking it apart) to combine.

5. Pour the batter into the prepared cake pan and smooth over the top. Bake in the oven for 45–47 minutes, until an inserted skewer comes out clean around the edges but may have some specks from the middle.

6. Leave to rest in the cake pan for 10 minutes, then carefully lift out onto a wire/cooling rack and leave to cool fully.

7. For the frosting, roughly mash the avocado flesh, then add to a small blender with the rest of the ingredients and blend until really smooth.

8. To finish the cake, place it on a serving plate, spread over the frosting, then decorate with the fresh berries or pomegranate seeds and chopped chocolate.

9. Eat straight away, or refrigerate in a sealed container for 3–5 days. It is best eaten at room temperature. You can freeze the unfrosted cake, covered tightly with cling film/plastic wrap, for 1 month, then defrost before decorating.

Healthy Brain ———— Snacks & Desserts

Top Tips
*If using gluten-free flour, add ½ tsp of xanthan gum to your flour if it doesn't already contain it, and use gluten-free baking powder. Squeeze out the excess moisture from the courgette, otherwise the cake will be too wet.

Tiramisu Chocolate Ganache Tart

Serves 10 | **Prep time:** 30 minutes + overnight soaking/chilling + 4 hours chilling

Who doesn't love the combination of coffee, cream and dark/bittersweet chocolate? This no-bake, plant-based and gluten-free tart is perfect for celebrations and sharing, and is made with healthful ingredients like oats, nuts and coconut cream. The natural caffeine boost is great for the brain, as it can stimulate our senses, help improve brain health and support cognition. Dark chocolate is also a powerhouse of antioxidants and flavonoids which aid learning and memory formation. This dessert is the ultimate pick-me-up (the literal translation of the word tira-mi-su).

Top Tips
When you chill a can of full-fat coconut milk in the refrigerator overnight, the solid and liquid parts will separate, then you can scoop out the solid part (cream), and use the liquid for another recipe. For the neatest slices, run a sharp knife under hot water, wipe it dry and slice the tart.

For the base

125g/4½oz/1¼ cups oat flour

100g/3½oz/1 cup almond flour

25g/1oz/¼ cup unsweetened cocoa powder

a pinch of salt

90g/3¼oz/3/8 cup runny smooth almond butter

2 tbsp maple syrup

2 tbsp melted coconut oil

2 tbsp brewed espresso coffee, cooled

½ tsp vanilla extract

For the ganache filling

180g/6¼oz/1½ cups raw cashew nuts

250g/9oz/1 cup coconut cream, taken from 1 x 400ml/14fl oz can full-fat coconut milk, chilled (see Top Tips)

170g/6oz dark/bittersweet chocolate, finely chopped

4 tbsp maple syrup

3 tbsp melted coconut oil

2 tbsp brewed espresso coffee, cooled

25g/1oz/¼ cup unsweetened cocoa powder

½ tsp vanilla extract

a pinch of salt

To serve

120ml/4fl oz/½ cup dairy-free whipping cream

1 tbsp unsweetened cocoa powder

coffee beans (optional)

1. First, prepare the cashews for the filling. Add the cashews to a large bowl and cover with cold water, then cover the bowl and leave to soak overnight. Alternatively, cover the cashews with boiling water and leave for 30 minutes to soften. Drain and rinse the cashews before using. Also, chill the can of coconut milk in the refrigerator overnight.

2. Grease the base and sides of a 20cm/8in loose-bottomed, shallow, round sandwich cake pan and line the base with baking parchment.

3. For the tart base, stir together the oat flour, almond flour, cocoa powder and salt in a large mixing bowl. Now add all the remaining ingredients and mix together to make a sticky dough. Transfer the mix to the lined cake pan and press down firmly to make a tart base and sides, working all the way up the sides. Refrigerate while you make the filling.

4. For the filling, melt the chocolate in a heatproof bowl, either in the microwave on High in 15-second bursts or over a pan of simmering water (known as a bain-marie), then allow it to cool down. Scoop off the solid cream part of the coconut milk in the can so you have the correct weight of coconut cream (save the rest for smoothies and curries).

5. Into a high-speed blender, add the soaked cashews, the coconut cream, melted chocolate and all the remaining filling ingredients. Blend until really creamy, stopping to scrape down the sides as necessary.

6. Remove the base from the refrigerator and pour in the ganache filling to reach the top of the tart base. Tap down on the surface to remove any air bubbles and return to the refrigerator for about 4 hours, or until set firm. If chilling overnight, cover tightly with cling film/plastic wrap.

7. Remove the tart from the refrigerator 30 minutes before serving and remove it from the tin (then leave it to rest for the 30 minutes). Whip the cream until fluffy and place in a piping/pastry bag with a round nozzle/tip (or similar).

8. To serve, pipe the cream over the tart, then sift over the cocoa powder. Decorate with coffee beans, if you like (but please don't eat them). Slice using a warmed sharp knife (see Top Tips) and serve, or keep covered in the refrigerator for 3–5 days. You can freeze the tart without the cream (once the tart is made, no need to wait for it to set) for 1 month, wrapped well, then defrost before decorating.

Espresso Walnut Cake Bars

Makes 9–12 | **Prep time:** 15 minutes + cooling | **Cook time:** 25 minutes

If you love a classic coffee and walnut cake, you are going to love this plant-based and brain-fuelling version. It is egg-free and comes with a luscious protein yogurt frosting. The antioxidant polyphenols in the coffee have a number of benefits such as lowering blood pressure, improving brain health and cognition and helping our brains as we age.

For the cake bars

1 large ripe banana

90g/3¼oz/3/8 cup thick coconut yogurt

60g/2¼oz/¼ cup runny smooth almond butter

75g/2¾oz/½ cup coconut sugar

2 tbsp espresso coffee, cooled

2 tbsp plant-based milk

1 tbsp ground chia seeds or ground flaxseed

1 tsp vanilla extract

140g/5oz/1 cup plain/all-purpose flour or gluten-free* plain/all-purpose flour

100g/3½oz/1 cup oat flour

½ tsp ground cinnamon

½ tsp bicarbonate of soda/baking soda

a pinch of salt

60g/2¼oz/½ cup walnuts, chopped

For the frosting

1 tbsp espresso coffee, cooled

180g/6¼oz/¾ cup thick coconut yogurt

3 tbsp vegan vanilla protein powder

1 tbsp maple syrup

To decorate

walnuts (some halves, some crushed)

coffee beans

ground cinnamon

1. Preheat the oven to 180°C/350°F/Gas 4 and line a 20cm/8in square baking pan with baking parchment.

2. In a large mixing bowl, mash the banana until smooth. Add the yogurt, almond butter, coconut sugar, espresso, milk, ground chia or flaxseed and vanilla and whisk until smooth.

3. Sift in the plain flour and then add the oat flour, cinnamon, bicarbonate of soda and salt. Stir to a thick, smooth batter with no lumps of flour. Fold in the walnuts.

4. Spoon the cake batter into the lined baking pan and smooth over the top. Bake in the oven for 22–25 minutes, until well-risen, golden on top and an inserted skewer comes out clean.

5. Allow the cake to cool in the baking pan for 10 minutes, then carefully turn it out and leave to cool fully on a wire/cooling rack.

6. Once cool, pierce the cake all over with a fork and brush over the 1 tbsp of espresso (for the frosting).

7. For the frosting, whisk together the yogurt, protein powder and maple syrup until smooth.

8. To decorate the cake, spread the frosting all over the cake and top with walnuts, coffee beans (only for decoration, please do not eat them) and a dusting of cinnamon. Slice the cake into 9 or 12 squares or bars. Enjoy!

9. Refrigerate leftover cake bars in a sealed container for 2–3 days. Or, you can freeze the unfrosted cake for 1 month, wrapped well, then defrost before brushing with the coffee and decorating with the frosting.

Top Tips

*When using gluten-free flour, ensure the flour contains xanthan gum, and if it doesn't, then add ½ tsp of xanthan gum to your flour blend for the cake bars mixture. If you fancy a more luxurious frosting, try the buttercream on page 203) without the lemon zest.

PART 2

happy
mind

CHAPTER 1

breakfast & brunch

Neapolitan Chia Pudding

Serves 4 | **Prep time:** 10 minutes + overnight soaking

Make-ahead breakfasts are a life-saver on busy mornings, and these colourful, creamy and delicious chia pudding jars will bring a smile to your face. They are layered with chocolate, strawberry and vanilla chia pudding mixtures that are made with simple, nutritious and mind-boosting foods. The omega-3 fatty acids in chia seeds are important for producing serotonin, while the raw cacao powder and strawberries contain polyphenols which feed our gut microbiome. Don't forget the coconut yogurt, too, which boosts gut bacteria, and we know that a healthy gut microbiome can support mood balance.

For the chocolate layer
300ml/10½fl oz/1¼ cups plant-based milk
4 tbsp thick coconut yogurt
2 tbsp maple syrup
2 tbsp raw cacao powder
a small pinch of salt
4 tbsp chia seeds

For the strawberry layer
160g/5¾oz/1 cup fresh strawberries, hulled
180ml/6fl oz/¾ cup plant-based milk
4 tbsp thick coconut yogurt
4 tbsp freeze-dried strawberry pieces (optional)
4 tbsp chia seeds

For the vanilla layer
300ml/10½floz/1¼ cups plant-based milk
4 tbsp thick coconut yogurt
½ tsp vanilla extract
4 tbsp chia seeds

To serve
4 fresh strawberries, halved
4 tbsp Brain Food Granola (see page 27)

1. For the chocolate layer, add a splash of the milk to a medium jar along with the coconut yogurt, maple syrup, cacao powder and salt. Whisk to a thick paste and then gradually pour in the rest of the milk, whisking until smooth. Now stir in the chia seeds and give it a good mix. Cover and leave to thicken in the refrigerator overnight.

2. For the strawberry layer, add the strawberries, milk, coconut yogurt and freeze-dried strawberries (if using) to a blender and blend until smooth. Pour into a second jar and stir in the chia seeds to combine. Cover and leave to thicken in the refrigerator overnight.

3. For the vanilla layer, stir together the milk, coconut yogurt and vanilla in a third jar until smooth. Now add the chia seeds and stir well. Cover and leave to thicken in the refrigerator overnight.

4. To serve, divide the chocolate chia pudding mix between four jars or bowls and top with the strawberry pudding mix and then the vanilla one. Serve with the strawberries and granola on top.

5. Eat straight away, or cover and refrigerate for 2–3 days.

Top Tip
Enjoy these chia puddings with extra fruit on top such as banana slices, blueberries, apple slices or orange segments. They're also great with chopped nuts or nut butter on top.

The Best Three Protein Smoothies

Serves 2 (each smoothie serves 2) | **Prep time:** 10 minutes (per smoothie)

Smoothies for breakfast are one of the best and quickest ways to start the day and are also delicious as a snack throughout the day. These are all loaded with mind-fuelling ingredients like omega-3-rich hemp seeds, coconut yogurt for the gut, plus a range of fruits and vegetables. The Mocha Date Shake is ideal for a little caffeine boost, the Mint Chocolate Chip Smoothie is fresh and vibrant with dark leafy spinach, fibre-rich dates and cacao nibs, which can help support serotonin production in the body, and the Peanut Butter and Berry Smoothie is loaded with antioxidants to look after the body and mind.

For the mocha date shake

- ½ courgette/zucchini, previously chopped and frozen
- 1 banana, previously sliced and frozen
- 1 Medjool date, pitted
- 2 tbsp hulled hemp seeds, plus extra to serve
- 2 tbsp thick coconut yogurt, plus extra to serve
- 2 tbsp runny smooth almond butter, plus extra to serve
- 240ml/8½fl oz/1 cup plant-based milk
- 1 shot (30ml or 2 tbsp) espresso coffee, hot or cold
- 1 scoop of vegan vanilla protein powder (optional)
- 2 tbsp cacao nibs (optional)

1. For the mocha date shake, add all the ingredients, except the cacao nibs (if using), to a blender and blend until smooth and creamy. Add some extra almond butter to two glasses, then pour in the smoothie. Top with some extra coconut yogurt, almond butter and hemp seeds and the cacao nibs (if using).

Top Tip

I love adding vegan vanilla protein powder to all of these smoothies, to make them thicker and creamier, plus it also adds a natural sweetness and vanilla flavour. These smoothies are also delicious without the protein powder, if preferred.

For the mint chocolate chip smoothie

a large handful of baby spinach

1 banana, previously sliced and frozen

2 large sprigs of fresh mint, leaves only, plus extra sprigs to serve

2 Medjool dates, pitted

2 tbsp hulled hemp seeds

2 tbsp thick coconut yogurt, plus extra to serve

240ml/8½fl oz/1 cup plant-based milk

1 scoop of vegan vanilla protein powder (optional)

2 tbsp cacao nibs, plus extra to serve

2. For the mint chocolate chip smoothie, add all the ingredients, except the cacao nibs, to a blender and process until creamy, smooth and vibrant. Now stir in the cacao nibs. Add some extra coconut yogurt to the base of two glasses, then pour in the smoothie. Top with more coconut yogurt, mint sprigs and cacao nibs.

For the peanut butter and berry smoothie

1 banana, previously sliced and frozen

100g/3½oz/½ cup frozen strawberries

70g/2½oz/½ cup frozen raspberries

2 tbsp hulled hemp seeds, plus extra to serve

2 tbsp thick coconut yogurt, plus extra to serve

2 tbsp runny smooth peanut butter, plus extra to serve

240ml/8½floz/1 cup plant-based milk

1 scoop of vegan vanilla protein powder (optional)

a handful of mixed fresh strawberries and raspberries

3. For the peanut butter and berry smoothie, add all the ingredients, except the fresh berries, to a blender and blend until thick and creamy. Add some extra peanut butter to two glasses, then pour in the smoothie. Top with extra coconut yogurt, the mixed fresh berries and some more peanut butter and hemp seeds.

4. All smoothies are best enjoyed straight away.

Banana Nut Cinnamon Rolls

Makes 6–8 | **Prep time:** 25 minutes + 20 minutes proofing + 30 minutes cooling | **Cook time:** 35 minutes

The smell of freshly baked cinnamon rolls in the morning just makes me smile; it's nostalgic, sweet, warming and whips up images of being sat around a fire or in a cosy coffee shop. These homemade rolls have had a glow-up with a pecan, walnut and banana cream cheese cinnamon filling, plus a protein yogurt frosting, while the dough also contains mashed banana. These are high in vitamin B6 which helps to synthesize feel-good hormones like dopamine and serotonin, and they are also great for the gut. Plus, these rolls contain no butter and less sugar, making them a wholesome plant-based and egg-free favourite.

Top Tips
These cinnamon rolls are delicious for brunch at the weekend or with a cup of tea or coffee in the afternoon, and are great for tearing and sharing. Please note, this recipe will not work with gluten-free flour.

For the dough

180ml/6¼fl oz/¾ cup
  plant-based milk

2 tbsp coconut oil

2 tbsp + 1 tsp olive oil,
  plus extra for greasing

2 tbsp coconut sugar

2¼ tsp (7g/⅛oz, or 1 sachet)
  fast-action dried yeast

175g/6oz/1¼ cups plain/
  all-purpose flour, plus
  extra for dusting

175g/6oz/1¼ cups strong
  white bread flour

1 tbsp ground cinnamon

1 tsp salt

60g/2¼oz/¼ cup
  mashed banana

For the filling

115g/4oz/½ cup vegan
  cream cheese

2 tbsp coconut sugar

1 tbsp ground cinnamon

1 tbsp cornflour/cornstarch

70g/2½oz/½ cup crushed
  mixed pecans and walnuts

1 banana, chopped
  into small chunks

For the frosting

120g/4¼oz/½ cup thick
  coconut yogurt

1 tbsp vegan cream cheese

2 tbsp vegan vanilla
  protein powder

1 tbsp plant-based
  milk (optional)

a sprinkling of ground
  cinnamon

1 tbsp crushed mixed
  pecans and walnuts

1 tbsp crushed banana
  chips/coins (dried
  banana slices)

1. Start by making the dough. Add the milk and coconut oil to a measuring jug and warm through in the microwave on Medium for 45–60 seconds, stirring every 15 seconds, until the coconut oil just melts (or do this in a saucepan). Whisk in 2 tbsp of the olive oil and the coconut sugar and check that the mix is lukewarm (you may need to let it cool down). Now sprinkle over the yeast and leave to activate for 5 minutes (it will start to become frothy and turn paler).

2. In a large bowl, whisk together both flours, the cinnamon and salt.

3. Pour the milky yeast mix into the flour, add the mashed banana and stir to a shaggy dough. Tip onto a lightly floured work surface and knead for 1–2 minutes to form a smooth ball of dough. Lightly grease a large mixing bowl and place the dough inside. Cover with a dish towel or cling film/plastic wrap and leave somewhere warm to rise for 20 minutes.

4. Preheat the oven to 180°C/350°F/Gas 4 and grease an ovenproof dish (approx. 24 x 18cm/9½ x 7in) with olive oil.

5. Make the filling by whisking together the cream cheese, coconut sugar, cinnamon and cornflour until smooth.

6. Lightly dust a work surface with more flour and tip out the risen dough. Roll out to a rectangle (approx. 36 x 30cm/14¼ x 12in). Spread over all the cream cheese filling, then sprinkle over the crushed nuts and chopped banana. Slice the rectangle lengthways into 6 or 8 even strips.

7. Roll up each strip into a cinnamon roll and place in the prepared ovenproof dish. Repeat to make all the rolls, placing them in the dish so they just touch each other. Lightly brush the rolls with the remaining 1 tsp of olive oil.

8. Bake in the oven for 30–35 minutes until well-risen and cooked through (you can test between the rolls to check the dough isn't wet). Leave the rolls to cool in the dish on a wire/cooling rack for 30 minutes (or cool fully and eat cold).

10. For the frosting, whisk together the yogurt, cream cheese and protein powder, adding the milk if needed to make it more spreadable. Spread the frosting over the rolls, then decorate with cinnamon, crushed nuts and banana chips. Remove from the dish and tear apart to serve. Eat straight away, or once cool, cover tightly with cling film/plastic wrap and refrigerate for 1 day. Serve at room temperature.

Apple, Date and Nut Breakfast Oat Cups

Makes 9–12 | **Prep Time:** 15 minutes + 30 minutes cooling | **Cook Time:** 20 minutes

These oat cups are my new favourite make-ahead breakfast (or as an afternoon snack with a cup of tea) and they make me so happy. They are full of gut-healthy yogurt, prebiotic-rich apples and dates and fibre-filled oats. All of these work to nourish the gut–brain axis, and the high fibre content enables the gradual release of sugar into the bloodstream to keep energy levels stable and stop us feeling "hangry" mid-morning!

For the oat cups

light olive oil spray, for greasing

120g/4¼oz/½ cup unsweetened shop-bought apple sauce

120g/4¼oz/½ cup thick coconut yogurt

60ml/2fl oz/¼ cup plant-based milk

60g/2¼oz/¼ cup smooth almond butter

3 tbsp maple syrup

1 tbsp coconut oil, melted

1 tbsp chia seeds

1 tsp vanilla extract

150g/5½oz/1½ cups rolled oats

½ tsp baking powder

½ tsp ground cinnamon

a pinch of salt

2 eating apples, cored, 1 finely chopped and 1 thinly sliced (2–3 slices per oat cup)

4 Medjool dates, pitted and roughly chopped

60g/2¼oz/½ cup walnuts, roughly chopped

Serving suggestions

extra thick coconut yogurt

extra smooth almond butter

fresh fruit and berries

1. Preheat the oven to 180°C/350°F/Gas 4 and grease 12 cupcake holes or 9 muffin holes in a cupcake/muffin pan with light olive oil spray. If you like, place two strips of thin baking parchment in a cross in each hole, so they overhang the edges to help lift out the cooked oat cups.

2. In a large mixing bowl, whisk together the apple sauce, coconut yogurt, milk, almond butter, 2 tbsp of the maple syrup, the coconut oil, chia seeds and vanilla until smooth. Now add in the oats, baking powder, cinnamon and salt and stir to a thick mix. Fold in the chopped apple, the dates and walnuts.

3. Use an ice-cream scoop or spoon to divide the mix evenly between the prepared cupcake or muffin holes, filling each to the top and pressing down to fill in all the gaps. Place the apple slices on top and brush them with the remaining maple syrup (this helps them to caramelize).

4. Bake in the oven for 20 minutes, or until golden brown and firm to touch.

5. Allow the cups to cool for 30 minutes in the cupcake/muffin pan and then use a palette knife/metal spatula to work all the way around each cup to ease them out.

6. Enjoy the oat cups warm or cold with extra coconut yogurt, almond butter and some fresh fruit, or on their own. They are also great cold. Refrigerate them in a sealed container for 3–5 days, or freeze for 1 month, then defrost before eating.

Top Tip
Make these nut-free by using sunflower seed butter or runny smooth tahini instead of almond butter, and swap the walnuts for mixed seeds.

Cinnamon Raisin Bagels and Garlic Chive Bagels
(No-yeast!)

Makes 6–8 | **Prep time:** 15 minutes + 10 minutes cooling | **Cook time:** 18 minutes

The smell of freshly-baked bagels is such a wonderful thing and now you can have the joy of making homemade bagels in less than 35 minutes. These bagels are just as fluffy, pillowy, soft and tasty as shop-bought bagels, but they are made without yeast and contain gut-loving coconut yogurt. The cinnamon raisin option is great for a sweet snack or breakfast with peanut butter and homemade chia-berry jam, and the garlic chive bagels are amazing with my No Nuts Homemade Cream Cheese (see page 198). They will make you so happy to eat and share with friends and family.

For the bagel base
(see Top Tips)

210g/7½oz/1½ cups self-
raising/self-rising flour*,
plus extra for dusting

240g/8½oz/1 cup thick
coconut yogurt

1 tsp salt

1 tbsp olive oil

For the cinnamon
raisin bagels

80g/2¾oz/½ cup raisins

2 tsp ground cinnamon

2 tbsp coconut sugar

2 tsp coconut oil, softened

1 tsp plain/all-
purpose flour*

For the garlic chive bagels

2 tbsp nutritional yeast

2 garlic cloves, crushed

1 tbsp chopped fresh chives

4 tbsp mixed white and
black sesame seeds

1. Preheat the oven to 180°C/350°F/Gas 4 and line a large baking sheet with baking parchment.

2. For the bagel base recipe, whisk together the flour, yogurt and salt in a large mixing bowl.

3. At this point, if making the cinnamon raisin bagels, stir in the raisins and 1 tsp of the cinnamon. Or, if making the garlic chive bagels, stir in the nutritional yeast, garlic and chives, and stir to a shaggy dough. Tip onto a lightly floured work surface and bring together with your hands by kneading for 1–2 minutes until smooth.

4. Roll out the dough to the thickness of your hand and use a cookie cutter (8cm/3¼in diameter) to cut out as many bagels as you can. Re-roll the scraps of dough to use all of it – you will make 6–8 bagels. Use a small round cutter (3cm/1¼in diameter) to cut a hole in the middle of each round of dough. Place all the bagels and the middles on the lined baking sheet.

5. For the cinnamon raisin topping, place the remaining 1 tsp of cinnamon and the rest of the ingredients into a small bowl and rub together with your fingers until crumbly.

6. Brush the bagels and bagel middles with the olive oil, then for the cinnamon raisin ones, sprinkle over the crumble topping. For the garlic chive bagels, sprinkle over the sesame seeds.

7. Bake in the oven for about 18 minutes until well-risen and golden. Turn the baking sheet around after 10 minutes, and remove the bagel middles at this time to a wire/cooling rack, as they will cook more quickly.

8. Leave the bagels to cool for 10 minutes before handling, then slice and enjoy warm with some peanut butter and chia-berry jam or homemade cream cheese.

9. Once cool, keep the bagels in a sealed container at room temperature for 1–2 days and enjoy cold, or you can slice and toast or grill/broil them until golden.

Top Tips
One quantity of the bagel base recipe is enough for one quantity of flavouring. *To make these gluten-free, use gluten-free self-raising flour and check if it contains xanthan gum. If it doesn't, add ½ tsp of xanthan gum. Use gluten-free plain flour for the cinnamon raisin option.

Chocolate Chip Peanut Butter Banana Bread

Serves 10 | **Prep time:** 20 minutes + cooling | **Cook time:** 50 minutes

Banana bread, chocolate and peanut butter are three of my favourite things and as part of my continued love for banana bread, I knew I wanted to include a brand-new, plant-based and nourishing recipe in this cookbook. This banana bread is moist, fluffy and spongy and contains so many mood-boosting ingredients like ripe banana (which is high in vitamin B6 to synthesize dopamine and serotonin), coconut yogurt (a fermented food known for its ability to support the gut–brain axis) and dark chocolate (a natural stimulant and high in polyphenols, which have a prebiotic effect and feed the gut). This super banana bread is great for sharing and ideal for brunch, snacking or dessert.

For the banana bread

80ml/2¾fl oz/⅓ cup
  plant-based milk

1 tbsp apple cider vinegar

3 ripe bananas (approx.
  300g/10½oz once mashed)

80g/2¾oz/⅓ cup runny
  smooth peanut butter

35g/1¼oz/¼ cup
  coconut sugar

2 tbsp thick coconut yogurt

1 tbsp ground flaxseed

1 tsp vanilla extract

210g/7½oz/1½ cups plain/
  all-purpose flour or
  gluten-free* plain/
  all-purpose flour

50g/1¾oz/½ cup
  ground almonds

½ tsp baking powder

½ tsp bicarbonate of
  soda/baking soda

a pinch of salt

85g/3oz dark/bittersweet
  chocolate chips

For the frosting

180g/6¼oz/¾ cup thick
  coconut yogurt

60g/2¼oz/¼ cup runny
  smooth peanut butter

2 tbsp vegan protein powder
  (e.g. vanilla or peanut
  flavour) (optional)

To decorate

2 tbsp runny smooth
  peanut butter

2 tbsp dark/bittersweet
  chocolate chips (or use
  your favourite chocolate
  bar, chopped, or even a
  homemade chocolate
  bar (see page 92)

2 tbsp crushed banana
  chips/coins (dried
  banana slices)

2 tbsp crushed roasted
  unsalted peanuts

1. Preheat the oven to 180°C/350°F/Gas 4. Grease and line a loaf pan (approx. 10 x 20cm/4 x 8in) with baking parchment.

2. In a measuring jug/pitcher, whisk together the milk and vinegar, then leave for 5 minutes to curdle. Mash the bananas well in a large mixing bowl.

3. Pour the milk mix into the mashed banana, then add the peanut butter, coconut sugar, coconut yogurt, ground flaxseed and vanilla and whisk until smooth.

4. Sift in the flour, then add the ground almonds, baking powder, bicarbonate of soda and salt and whisk again to a smooth, thick batter.

5. Fold in the chocolate chips, then pour into the prepared loaf pan and smooth over the top. Bake in the oven for 48–50 minutes until well-risen, golden on top and an inserted skewer comes out clean (small specks of wetness are okay).

6. Cool in the loaf pan for 10 minutes, then carefully lift out onto a wire/cooling rack and leave to cool fully.

7. For the frosting, whisk together all the ingredients in a bowl until smooth and thick. Spread the frosting all over the cooled cake.

8. To decorate, swirl on the peanut butter, then sprinkle over the chocolate chips, crushed banana chips/coins and crushed peanuts.

9. Slice and serve straight away, or refrigerate in a sealed container for 3–5 days and eat at room temperature. You can freeze the unfrosted loaf, wrapped well in cling film/plastic wrap, for 1 month, then defrost before decorating.

Top Tips

The riper the bananas, the better, as they are naturally sweeter and easier to mash.
*When using gluten-free flour, ensure the blend contains xanthan gum, and if it doesn't, then add ½ tsp of xanthan gum to your flour (and use gluten-free baking powder).

Pear and Walnut Streusel Muffins

Makes 10–12 | **Prep time:** 15 minutes + cooling | **Cook time:** 25 minutes

For the streusel top

25g/1oz/¼ cup walnuts, finely chopped

35g/1¼oz/¼ cup plain/ all-purpose or spelt flour or gluten-free* plain/ all-purpose flour

2 tbsp coconut sugar

2 tbsp coconut oil, slightly softened

For the muffins

2 small pears (approx. 150g/5½oz/1 cup)

80ml/2¾fl oz/⅓ cup plant-based milk

½ tbsp apple cider vinegar or lemon juice

240g/8½oz/1 cup unsweetened apple sauce

100g/3½oz/½ cup coconut sugar

80ml/2¾fl oz/⅓ cup light olive oil

1 tsp vanilla extract

280g/10oz/2 cups plain/ all-purpose or spelt flour or gluten-free* plain/ all-purpose flour

1 tsp ground cinnamon

½ tsp ground ginger

2 tsp baking powder

⅓ tsp bicarbonate of soda/baking soda

a pinch of salt

50g/1¾oz/½ cup walnuts, finely chopped

For the glaze

60g/2¼oz/½ cup icing/ confectioners' sugar

1½–2 tsp plant-based milk

These tempting muffins are made with gut-loving ingredients like apple cider vinegar, prebiotic-rich fruits and omega-3-rich walnuts, which is key for brain health/ mood support. They are tender, light and fluffy and will rival your favourite bakery with high muffin tops!

1. Preheat the oven to 180°C/350°F/Gas 4 and line a muffin pan with 10–12 paper muffin cases/liners. If making bakery-style high-top muffins like these ones, you will make 10, otherwise, make 12 slightly smaller muffins.

2. For the streusel top, add the walnuts to a small mixing bowl with the flour and coconut sugar. Stir, then add in the coconut oil and rub in with your fingers to make a crumbly consistency. Leave to one side.

3. Prepare the pears for the muffins by slicing the fruit, removing the core and chopping into small chunks.

4. Stir together the milk and vinegar or lemon juice in a small glass and allow to rest for 5 minutes to curdle (this helps to bind the mix).

5. In a large mixing bowl, whisk together the milk mix, the apple sauce, coconut sugar, olive oil and vanilla. Sift in the flour, cinnamon, ginger, baking powder and bicarbonate of soda. Add the salt and whisk to a thick batter.

6. Fold in the chopped pears and walnuts with a spoon.

7. Divide the mix equally between the cases. If making 10 muffins, fill them to the top. Sprinkle over the streusel mix.

8. Bake in the oven for 25 minutes (or 22–25 minutes for 12 smaller muffins) until well-risen, fluffy and an inserted skewer comes out clean.

9. Leave to cool for 5 minutes before carefully removing from the muffin pan to cool fully on a wire/cooling rack.

10. Stir together the icing sugar and milk for the glaze and drizzle over the muffins. Enjoy straight away, or refrigerate in a sealed container for 3–5 days. You can also freeze for 1 month, then defrost before eating.

Top Tip

*When using gluten-free flour, ensure the blend contains xanthan gum, and if it doesn't, then add ½ tsp of xanthan gum to your flour for the muffin mix (and use gluten-free baking powder).

Strawberry Cheesecake French Toast

Serves 4 (makes 8 slices) | **Prep time:** 20 minutes + 10 minutes soaking | **Cook time:** 25 minutes

French toast is a classic for brunch at the weekend with friends or family. This mood-boosting recipe is so delicious and fun. It has an egg-free, healthier batter made using banana, which acts as a natural sweetener, and chia seeds which are high in omega-3 fatty acids. Inspired by strawberry cheesecake, this brunch dish includes gooey, sticky strawberries, a homemade cookie crumb topping and a coconut yogurt "cheesecake" mix. Add on some sprinkles to take these to the next level.

Top Tip
You can prepare the French toast ahead of time, with all the components, then warm back up to serve, so you can be the hostess with the most-ess for brunch gatherings!

For the French toast

1 ripe banana

*320ml/11¼fl oz/1⅓ cups
plant-based milk*

*2 tbsp melted and
cooled coconut oil,
plus extra (melted)
for baking or frying*

2 tbsp chia seeds

1 tsp ground cinnamon

1 tsp vanilla extract

*8 slices of fresh bread
of your choice (I used
a white bloomer)*

For the cookie crumb

50g/1¾oz/½ cup oat flour

1 tbsp coconut flour

½ tbsp maple syrup

½ tbsp melted coconut oil

*½ tbsp runny smooth
almond butter*

For the gooey strawberries

*320g/11¼oz/2 heaped
cups fresh strawberries,
chopped*

2 tsp lemon juice

2 tsp maple syrup

For the cheesecake yogurt

*240g/8½oz/1 cup thick
coconut yogurt*

2 tsp lemon juice

1 tbsp maple syrup

To serve

4 fresh strawberries, halved

*2 tbsp sprinkles of
your choice*

*4 tbsp maple syrup
(optional)*

1. Start by making the French toast batter. Add the banana, milk, coconut oil, chia seeds, cinnamon and vanilla to a small blender and blend until smooth. Pour the mix into a shallow dish, then dip in each of the bread slices, so the batter coats both sides. Leave the bread to soak for 10 minutes.

2. Meanwhile, to make the cookie crumb, stir together all the ingredients into a crumbly mix in a small bowl. Pour into a large non-stick frying pan and cook over a high heat for 5 minutes, stirring often, until crispy, temove from the pan and set aside.

3. Next, prepare the gooey strawberries. Add all the ingredients to a small saucepan and bubble away over a high heat for 5 minutes until sticky and saucy.

4. If you are going to bake the French toast, preheat the oven to 180°C/350°F/Gas 4 and line a large baking sheet with baking parchment.

5. Once the bread has soaked, allow any excess batter to drip off, then brush each side with coconut oil and place on the lined baking sheet, ensuring they do not overlap. Bake in the oven for 10 minutes, then carefully flip over and bake for another 10 minutes, until golden brown and soft.

6. Alternatively, to fry the French toast, heat a large non-stick frying pan with some coconut oil, and once hot, place the battered bread in the pan (as many as you can fit) and fry over a medium-high heat for 3–5 minutes until golden brown, then carefully flip over to cook the second side (for about 3 minutes). Repeat to make all eight slices, keeping them warm on a baking sheet in the oven at the lowest setting.

7. For the cheesecake yogurt, stir together all the ingredients until combined.

8. To serve, stack two slices of French toast on each plate and top with some cheesecake yogurt, gooey strawberries and cookie crumb. Add on two strawberry halves, some sprinkles, and a drizzle of maple syrup, if you like.

9. Enjoy straight away, or once cool, refrigerate the components in separate containers for 2–3 days. Warm the French toast back up in a frying pan and warm the strawberries in a saucepan until bubbling to serve.

Chocolate Banana Oat Flour Crêpes

Serves 4 (makes 16–20 crêpes) | **Prep time:** 15 minutes | **Cook time:** 30 minutes

Crêpes are one of life's little joys and they are simple and quick to make, especially without eggs, dairy or gluten. These family-friendly, crowd-pleasing, delicious oat and buckwheat flour crêpes are loaded with gut-healthy ingredients like banana, ground flaxseed and hazelnuts, which is great for increasing the diversity of our microbiome. Plus the homemade chocolate hazelnut "nutella" will make everyone happy, as it's creamy, chocolatey and so indulgent and is great spooned from the jar.

For the crêpe batter

100g/3½oz/1 cup oat flour or rolled oats

70g/2½oz/½ cup buckwheat flour

2 tbsp ground flaxseed

1 tsp ground cinnamon

360ml/12½fl oz/1½ cups plant-based milk

1 ripe banana

2 tbsp hazelnut butter

2 tbsp maple syrup

a pinch of salt

olive or coconut oil, for frying

For the homemade "nutella"

120g/4¼oz/½ cup hazelnut butter

85g/3oz dairy-free milk chocolate, finely chopped

For the filling

240g/8½oz/1 cup thick coconut yogurt

2 bananas, sliced

4 tbsp chopped chocolate of your choice

4 tbsp chopped raw blanched hazelnuts

1. Start by making the crêpe batter. Add all the ingredients, except the oil for frying, to a blender and blend until smooth. Leave for 5 minutes to thicken.

2. Meanwhile, make the "nutella" by adding the hazelnut butter and milk chocolate to a heatproof bowl, then heat in the microwave on High for about 45–60 seconds, stirring every 15 seconds, until melted and glossy. While warm, the "nutella" is runny, but will thicken as it cools, so warm it up in 15-second bursts as needed. Store leftovers in a sealed container at room temperature for 1–2 weeks.

3. Heat a large non-stick pan with a little olive or coconut oil, and once hot, add some of the crêpe batter (I use a spoon or ladle) and quickly swirl it around to make a round shape (as big or as small as you like; I suggest each is about 13cm/5in diameter, and cook a couple at a time, if they fit, or use two pans). Cook over a medium-high heat for 2 minutes until the batter looks dry on top and it starts to bubble. Use a spatula (or angled palette knife/metal spatula) to flip it over and then cook the second side for 1 minute. Remove to a plate. Repeat to make all the crêpes (you'll make 16–20 crêpes), adding a little extra oil as needed.

4. Keep the cooked crêpes warm in a low oven, covered with foil, while you cook the remainder.

5. To serve the crêpes, spread them with some coconut yogurt, then top with the banana slices and homemade "nutella". Add on some chopped chocolate and hazelnuts, fold loosely and enjoy warm.

6. Refrigerate leftover un-filled crêpes in a sealed container for 2–3 days, or wrap in cling film/plastic wrap and freeze for 1 month. Defrost and eat cold or warm up in a frying pan.

Top Tips

The crêpes can also be filled with any other toppings you like; for example, fresh berries and thick coconut yogurt, nut butter and jam, lemon juice and coconut sugar, or with my Rhubarb and Ginger (see Brain Booster Creamy Oats Three Ways recipe on page 41).

Caramelized Peach and Vanilla Pancakes

Serves 4 (makes 16 smaller American-style pancakes) | **Prep time:** 15 minutes | **Cook time:** 20 minutes

It's hard to beat waking up to pancakes at the weekend, and these delicious sticky pancake stacks are made with good-for-you ingredients everyone will adore. The oats are great for a slow release of energy, which is important for maintaining a happy mood and preventing those "hangry feelings, while the vitamin B6 in bananas helps to synthesize feel-good hormones like serotonin. These pancakes will make you feel amazing and they taste even better.

For the pancakes

150g/5½oz/1½ cups
    rolled oats

140g/5oz/1 cup plain/
    all-purpose flour

1 tsp ground cinnamon

1 tbsp chia seeds

240ml/8½fl oz/1 cup
    plant-based milk

2 ripe bananas

1 tbsp maple syrup

1 tsp baking powder

1 tsp vanilla extract

a pinch of salt

coconut, avocado or
    olive oil, for frying

For the caramelized peaches

6 ripe peaches

2 tbsp maple syrup

To serve

4 tbsp thick coconut yogurt

2 tbsp crushed pistachios

1. Start by preparing the pancake batter. Add all the ingredients to a blender and blend together until smooth. Leave to rest for 10 minutes while you prepare the peaches.

2. Slice the peaches in half, removing the pits, then slice the halves into thin slices (1cm/½in thickness) until you have 16 slices. Chop the rest of the peaches into small chunks and place these in a small saucepan, then set aside.

3. Work in batches to make the pancakes, keeping them warm on a plate under a dish towel once cooked. Heat a large non-stick frying pan with a little oil, and once hot, add about three peach slices (or as many as the pan allows – to make a small pancake with each slice) and fry off over a medium-high heat for 1 minute. Now spoon some pancake batter over each piece of peach to cover it around the sides (keeping each one separate in the pan – like you would do if making Scotch pancakes). Cook for 2 minutes, or until golden underneath and there are some bubbles on top. Flip over and cook on the other side for 2 minutes, or until well-risen and cooked through. Remove from the pan and keep warm, then repeat to make all the pancakes.

5. Meanwhile, place the saucepan of peach chunks over a high heat. Add the maple syrup. Cook for 5 minutes, stirring occasionally to soften the fruit and make them really sticky.

6. To serve, stack the warm pancakes up on plates and serve with the coconut yogurt and sticky peach chunks. Finish with the crushed pistachios. Eat straight away. Or, refrigerate leftover cooked pancakes (without toppings) in a sealed container for 2–3 days, or freeze for 1 month, then defrost (if frozen) and warm back up in a frying pan for a few minutes to serve. Refrigerate leftover caramelized peaches in a separate sealed container for 2–3 days and warm through to serve.

Top Tips
You can use other fruits instead of peaches, like nectarines, apples, plums or pears, to caramelize and top with the pancake batter.

CHAPTER 2

lunch

Veggie Edamame Fried Rice with Sticky Tofu

Serves 4 | **Prep Time:** 10 minutes + 10 minutes (or 1–2 hours) marinating | **Cook Time:** 20 minutes

This vibrant, nourishing spin on a classic fried rice recipe always makes me feel happy. The tofu is golden and sticky thanks to a lovely umami marinade, the rice is packed with an array of antioxidants, vitamins and minerals from all the vegetables, and the brown rice provides fibre-rich wholegrain goodness. All these ingredients can enhance the gut-brain axis, as well as reduce stress and improve digestion.

For the tofu and marinade

4 tbsp tamari soy sauce

2 tbsp sesame seed oil

2 tsp brown rice miso paste

juice of 2 limes, plus wedges to serve

2 tbsp maple syrup

2 x 200g/7oz blocks of extra-firm tofu, drained and cut into cubes

For the fried rice

200g/7oz/1 cup long-grain brown rice

2 tbsp sesame oil

2 large spring onions/scallions, thinly sliced

3 garlic cloves, crushed

a thumb-size piece of root ginger, peeled and grated

½ red chilli, finely diced (optional), plus extra to serve

2 carrots, washed and thinly sliced

300g/10½oz/2 cups broccoli, finely chopped

1 large red pepper, deseeded and thinly sliced

300g/10½oz/2 cups frozen edamame beans, defrosted

3 tbsp chopped fresh herbs (e.g. basil, coriander/chives or chives)

2 tbsp mixed sesame seeds

1. Start by making the tofu marinade. In a large mixing bowl, stir together all the ingredients (apart from the tofu) until combined. Toss the tofu in the marinade. Leave to marinate for 10 minutes (or you can make this 1–2 hours before, cover and refrigerate).

2. Cook the rice according to the package directions, drain and leave to one side.

3. When the rice has about 10 minutes to go, heat 1 tbsp of the sesame oil in a large non-stick pan, and once hot, spoon in the tofu cubes (leaving the marinade in the bowl). Cook over a high heat, tossing regularly, until the tofu is turning crispy and dark golden in colour, about 5 minutes. Remove the tofu from the pan.

4. Add the remaining sesame oil to the pan, then add the spring onions, garlic, ginger and chilli and fry over a high heat for 1 minute until fragrant. Now add in the carrots, broccoli and red pepper. Continue to fry for 5 minutes, to soften the vegetables but so they retain a bite. Add in the edamame beans, cooked rice, most of the tofu, the rest of the marinade and most of the herbs.

5. Heat through for a few minutes before dividing between four bowls and topping with the rest of the tofu and herbs. Sprinkle with the sesame seeds and extra chilli slices and serve with lime wedges.

6. Enjoy straight away, or allow to cool, refrigerate in a sealed container for 1–2 days, then warm back up in a pan before eating.

Top Tip

You can swap the vegetables in this recipe for whatever you have at home. Try different coloured peppers, swap the carrots for red cabbage and the broccoli for courgettes/zucchini or mushrooms.

Nutty Pea Quinoa Hummus Bowls

Serves 4 | **Prep time:** 10 minutes | **Cook time:** 15 minutes

Ready in 25 minutes, these tasty hummus bowls are vibrant and packed with flavour and crunch and they are so easy to make for a midweek lunch or dinner. They are topped with tamari Brazil nuts, naturally high in selenium, which supports brain function, and the abundance of greens provide polyphenols, which nourish the gut microbiome, so are hugely beneficial for our gut.

For the herby hummus

1 x 400g/14oz can
chickpeas/garbanzo
beans or cannellini
beans (240g/8½oz/1½
cups once drained,
but keep the liquid)

60g/2¼oz/¼ cup runny
smooth tahini

3 bunches of fresh herbs
(e.g. basil, mint and/
or coriander/cilantro)

juice of 1 lemon

2 tbsp extra virgin olive oil

1 garlic clove, peeled

salt and pepper, to taste

For the nutty pea quinoa

200g/7oz/1 cup tri-
colour quinoa

2 tbsp tamari soy sauce

70g/2½oz/¼ cup
Brazil nuts, halved

2 tbsp olive oil

2 large spring onions/
scallions, thinly sliced

4 garlic cloves, sliced

160g/5¾oz/2 cups
broccoli, finely chopped

100g/3½oz/4 cups cavolo
nero or kale (de-stemmed
weight), shredded

200g/7oz/1½ cups frozen
peas, defrosted

2 tbsp chopped fresh mixed
herbs (e.g. basil, mint
and coriander/cilantro)

juice of 1 lime

To serve

red chilli slices (optional)

a few sprigs of fresh
coriander/cilantro
and/or mint

1 spring onion/scallion,
thinly sliced

lime wedges

1. Start by making the herby hummus. Drain the chickpeas or beans, keeping the liquid from the can to one side. Add the chickpeas or beans to a food processor or blender with 60ml/2fl oz/¼ cup of the reserved liquid. Add in all the other ingredients and blend until really smooth, adding 1–2 tbsp more of the reserved liquid, as needed. Scoop into a container, cover and refrigerate for 2–3 days (if making in advance).

2. Cook the quinoa according to the package directions, then leave to one side.

3. Meanwhile, add 1 tbsp of the tamari and the Brazil nuts to a large non-stick frying pan and warm them through over a medium-high heat, stirring well, until evenly coated, then cook for 1–2 minutes until smelling fragrant. Transfer to a small bowl.

4. Using the same pan (no need to clean it out), heat up the olive oil. Once hot, add the spring onions and garlic and fry off over a high heat for 2 minutes, to soften the onions. Now add the broccoli, kale and a large pinch of salt with some black pepper and cook over a medium-high heat for 3 minutes. The broccoli will retain some bite.

5. Stir in the peas, chopped herbs, quinoa, the second tbsp of tamari and the lime juice. Allow to warm through for a couple of minutes.

6. To serve, spread some herby hummus onto four plates and pile high with the quinoa mix. Add on the tamari Brazil nuts and serve with chilli slices (if using), herb sprigs, spring onion slices and lime wedges.

7. Enjoy straight away, or allow the quinoa mix to cool, then refrigerate in a separate sealed container for 2–3 days. Keep the tamari Brazil nuts in a small sealed container at room temperature for 2–3 days.

Top Tip

You can add any other vegetables into this quinoa mix like sliced courgette/ zucchini, deseeded red pepper or mushrooms.

Hidden Vegetable Squash and Tomato Soup

Serves 4 as a main, serves 6 as a starter or small plate
Prep time: 15 minutes | **Cook time:** 40 minutes

This soup is my favourite way to sneak a variety of plants into my meal as well as lots of protein, fibre and antioxidants. This warming bowl of soup is nostalgic, comforting and so warming, making it the perfect winter warmer, served with some herbs and seeds on top and your favourite bread to accompany. You'd never tell there's so much goodness in every bowl!

For the soup

1 large butternut squash, peeled, deseeded and cut into small cubes (you will have about 800–900g/1lb 12oz–2lb/5–5½ cups)

4 large beefsteak tomatoes, halved

1 large carrot, washed and chopped into chunks

1 red pepper, deseeded and roughly chopped

1 tsp ground cumin

½ tsp ground turmeric

½ tsp hot smoked paprika

3 tbsp olive oil

1 garlic bulb

1 x 400g/14oz can cannellini beans, drained and rinsed (240g/8½oz/1½ cups drained weight)

1 x 400ml/14oz can full-fat or light coconut milk

a thumb-size piece of root ginger, peeled and roughly chopped

1 tbsp brown rice miso paste

salt and pepper, to taste

To serve

4–6 tbsp thick coconut yogurt

fresh herbs (e.g. coriander/ cilantro, parsley or basil)

4–6 tbsp sunflower seeds

1. Preheat the oven to 200°C/400°F/Gas 6 and line a large baking sheet with baking parchment.

2. Add all the vegetables to the lined baking sheet with the spices and some salt and pepper, then drizzle over 2½ tbsp of the olive oil. Toss well with your hands.

3. Trim the top off the garlic bulb and remove any excess skin, so that the cloves are still covered but the paper skin is torn off. Place the garlic in the middle of the baking sheet and drizzle over the remaining ½ tbsp of olive oil.

4. Roast the vegetables in the oven for 30–40 minutes, until tender and smelling fragrant. You can toss them halfway through cooking, so they cook evenly.

5. Allow the vegetables to cool slightly, then squeeze 3–4 large garlic cloves out of their skins onto the baking sheet (save the leftover garlic for other recipes!). Add all the vegetables, their juices and the squeezed out garlic cloves to a blender with the beans, coconut milk, ginger, miso and 120ml/4fl oz/½ cup water. Blend until really creamy, adding more water if needed (you may need to blend in batches).

6. Add the soup to a large saucepan to warm back through and then serve in bowls with a swirl of coconut yogurt, some fresh herbs and the sunflower seeds. I also like this with hunks of fresh bread.

7. Cool any leftovers, then refrigerate in a sealed container for 2–3 days, or freeze for 1 month. Gently warm back up (from chilled or frozen) to eat.

Top Tips

You can mix up the vegetables here: try swapping squash for pumpkin or sweet potatoes and add in courgette/zucchini or parsnips, too. Also, you can swap out the cannellini beans for butter/lima beans or chickpeas/garbanzo beans.

Rainbow Vegetable Tofu Wraps

Serves 4 (makes 8 wraps) | **Prep time:** 10 minutes | **Cook time:** 10 minutes (optional)

These rainbow wraps will make you so happy. Not only are they fresh, vibrant and delicious, but they are also ready in 10 or 20 minutes, making them a quick and easy lunch for busy workdays or to enjoy on-the-go. They will nourish your mind all day long with omega-3-rich hemp seeds, high-protein homemade hummus and gut-healthy tofu. The abundance of colour in these wraps makes them nutrient-rich, as different coloured vegetables contain a variety of vitamins and minerals, so these really do feed your mind.

For the wraps

8 spring/collard greens leaves

2 x 200g/7oz blocks extra-firm tofu, drained

1 tbsp olive oil (optional)

1 small cucumber

1 large carrot, washed

1 red pepper, deseeded

1 quantity of Homemade Hummus (see page 159)

80g/2¾oz/½ cup sun-dried tomatoes from a jar (drained weight), cut in half if large

4 handfuls of fresh sprouted seeds or grains

4 sprigs of fresh mint, leaves only

2 tbsp hulled hemp seeds

salt and pepper, to taste

1. Wash the spring greens leaves and trim off the stiff stems at the bottom.

2. Pat the tofu dry and slice into 10cm/4in pieces. The tofu is great to eat raw, or you can pan-fry it now. Heat a large non-stick frying pan with the olive oil, and once hot, add the tofu strips with some salt and pepper. Fry over a high heat for 5–10 minutes so they turn golden and start to crisp on all sides. Now remove from the pan.

3. Chop the cucumber, carrot and red pepper into similar-size matchsticks to the tofu.

4. To prepare the wraps, place each green leaf on a chopping board and spoon over some hummus in the middle, then top with some tofu strips, sun-dried tomatoes and the cucumber, carrot and red pepper strips. Sprinkle over some sprouted seeds/grains, mint leaves and hemp seeds and season with black pepper.

5. Like you'd wrap a tortilla, lift the bottom of each leaf up and over the filling, tucking the sides in as you roll the leaf forward to seal it into a wrap. Slice in half with a large, sharp knife, and enjoy.

6. Eat straight away, or refrigerate in a sealed container for 2–3 days.

Top Tip
You can also make these wraps using wholemeal/whole-wheat or seedy soft flour tortilla wraps instead of the green leaves, using the filling as above.

Kimchi Edamame Satay Bowls

Serves 4 | **Prep time:** 10 minutes | **Cook time:** 15 minutes

For the bowls

200g/7oz/1 cup brown rice
(short- or long-grain)

160g/5¾oz/1¾ cups red
cabbage, shredded

juice of ½ lime

a pinch of salt

300g/10½oz/1 cup
frozen edamame
beans, defrosted

1 large carrot, washed
and grated

4 radishes, thinly sliced

2 spring onions/
scallions, thinly sliced

1 ripe avocado, peeled,
pitted and sliced

4 tbsp kimchi

2 tbsp mixed white and
black sesame seeds

2 tbsp crushed nori
(optional)

½ red chilli, thinly sliced

a handful of fresh
mint, leaves only

4 lime wedges

For the satay sauce

4 tbsp runny smooth
peanut butter

2 tbsp tamari soy sauce

1 tbsp sriracha hot sauce

juice of 1 lime

1 tsp light brown rice
miso paste

2 garlic cloves, crushed

a small thumb-size
piece of root ginger,
peeled and grated

4 tbsp full-fat coconut milk
(from a can or carton)

salt and pepper, to taste

These vibrant and wholesome satay bowls are the ideal lunch to make ahead. They come together in minimal time with maximum flavour, thanks to the delicious miso peanut satay sauce, which is great for adding gut-friendly fermented foods into your diet. The addition of kimchi increases your probiotic bacteria, which supports the gut-brain axis and may even help to support your mood. Also, the phytochemicals in the avocado may help to reduce stress.

1. Start by cooking the rice according to the package directions (usually around 15 minutes).

2. Meanwhile, for the quick pickled cabbage, add the shredded red cabbage to a small bowl with the lime juice and the pinch of salt. Massage with your hands for 30 seconds, to soften the cabbage. Set aside.

3. For the satay sauce, whisk together all the ingredients, apart from the coconut milk, in a small bowl until smooth, then gradually whisk in the coconut milk to reach a pourable consistency. Season to taste with salt and pepper.

4. To serve, divide the cooked hot rice between four bowls and top with the edamame beans, quick pickled cabbage, carrot, radishes, spring onions, avocado and kimchi. Pour over the satay sauce and then top with the sesame seeds, crushed nori (if using), chilli slices and fresh mint. Add a wedge of lime to each bowl.

5. Enjoy straight away, or refrigerate leftovers in a sealed container for 2–3 days and eat cold.

Top Tip

You can play around with the colours in this bowl by switching up the vegetables; for example, try white cabbage instead of red, and swap the radishes for chopped mangetout/snow peas.

Kale Caesar Salad with Crispy Tofu

Serves 4 | **Prep time:** 15 minutes | **Cook time:** 25 minutes

This recipe has everything we all know and love about the classic Caesar salad – crunchy greens, a creamy tangy dressing and some delicious protein. Yet, this salad has had a major upgrade with golden crispy tofu, roasted broccoli and the best super-smooth and high-protein Caesar dressing (without any mayonnaise). This will bring back fond memories while nourishing the gut–brain axis. The range of prebiotic-rich vegetables feed the friendly bacteria in the gut, the dark leafy greens contain magnesium to boost mood, while the avocado helps the stress response. Overall, this is a winning lunch.

For the crispy tofu

1 tbsp olive oil

1 tbsp tamari soy sauce

1 garlic clove, crushed

*2 x 200g/7oz blocks of
extra-firm tofu, drained,
patted dry and cut
into small cubes*

*16 stems of long-stem
broccoli (approx.
320g/11¼oz), trimmed*

*4 slices of wholemeal/
whole-wheat, sourdough
or seedy bread,
chopped into cubes*

salt and pepper, to taste

For the Caesar dressing

*1 x 300g/10½oz
block of silken tofu,
drained (290g/10¼oz
drained weight)*

6 tbsp thick coconut yogurt

4 tbsp nutritional yeast

2 garlic cloves, crushed

1 tbsp apple cider vinegar

1 tsp Dijon mustard

1 tsp capers

For the salad

*100g/3½oz/4 cups cavolo
nero or kale (de-stemmed
weight), roughly chopped*

1 tsp olive oil

a pinch of salt

*4 handfuls of salad greens
of your choice (e.g. baby
spinach, watercress,
rocket/arugula)*

*2 spring onions/
scallions, sliced*

*1 ripe avocado, peeled,
pitted and sliced*

*a large sprig of fresh
basil, leaves only*

*4 tbsp Homemade Vegan
Parmesan (see page 81)*

1. Preheat the oven to 180°C/350°F/Gas 4 and line a large baking sheet with baking parchment.

2. While the oven preheats, prep the crispy tofu. In a small mixing bowl, whisk together the olive oil, tamari, garlic and some salt and pepper until combined. Add the tofu cubes, stir gently to mix and leave for 10 minutes.

3. Spoon the tofu from the marinade bowl and spread it out on the lined baking sheet (leaving the marinade behind). Bake in the oven for 10 minutes. Add the broccoli and bread cubes into the marinade and toss. After 10 minutes of the tofu cooking, add the broccoli and bread to the baking sheet and return to the oven for another 10–15 minutes until the tofu is golden, the broccoli is crisping and the bread is crunchy. Ensure nothing overlaps for even cooking.

4. Meanwhile, prepare the dressing by blending together all the ingredients with some salt and pepper in a blender or food processor until smooth. This will keep in a sealed container in the refrigerator for 2–3 days, if you make it in advance.

5. For the salad, add the kale to a large bowl with the olive oil and the pinch of salt. Massage with your hands for 30 seconds, to wilt the leaves. Now add in the salad greens, spring onions and most of the dressing and toss well.

6. When everything has finished roasting, tip half of the roasted mixture into the salad bowl and toss again.

7. Divide the salad between four plates or bowls and top with some extra spoonfuls of dressing. Spoon over the remaining roasted mixture, then add the avocado, basil leaves and vegan parmesan.

8. Enjoy straight away, or refrigerate the salad in a sealed container for 1–2 days. If you can, keep the croutons separately so they stay crisp, then toss through before eating (add the avocado, basil and vegan parmesan just before serving, too).

Top Tip

You can use your favourite bread here, but I also like to use my Superfood Buckwheat land Seed Bread (see page 95).

Beetroot Hummus with Lentils and Pistachios

Serves 4 as a main; serves 6 as a starter or small plate | **Prep time:** 15 minutes | **Cook time:** 5 minutes

This requires very little effort but gives maximum satisfaction – it just makes me so happy to look at. The vibrant pink hummus is loaded with antioxidant-rich beetroot/beet, fibre- and protein-rich chickpeas/garbanzo beans and healthy monounsaturated fats from the olive oil. All these support a happy gut, which in turn contributes to a healthy gut–brain axis, while tahini, made from sesame seeds, also contains tryptophan, an amino acid responsible for producing mood-boosting serotonin. It's a great dish to share with friends and family!

For the hummus

1 x 400g/14oz can
  chickpeas, drained and
  rinsed (240g/8½oz/1½
  cups drained weight)

170g/6oz (about 2) cooked
  beetroots/beets (in natural
  juice, not vinegar), drained
  and roughly chopped

4 tbsp runny smooth tahini

2 tbsp extra virgin olive oil

2 tbsp lemon juice

1 garlic clove, peeled

1 tsp ground cumin

salt and pepper, to taste

For the lentils and pistachios

50g/1¾oz/⅓ cup
  shelled pistachios

½ tsp fennel seeds

½ tsp cumin seeds

120g/4¼oz/¾ cup
  cooked Puy lentils

3 large sprigs of fresh mint,
  leaves very finely chopped

grated zest of ½ lemon

½ tbsp lemon juice

½ tbsp extra virgin olive oil

To serve

2 tbsp extra virgin olive oil

a large sprig of fresh
  mint, leaves only

4–6 pitta breads, toasted

1. Start by making the hummus. Add the chickpeas and all the other ingredients to a food processor or blender and blend until really smooth. Stop to scrape down the sides as needed, and season to taste with salt and pepper. Pour into a sealable container and refrigerate until ready to use. It will keep (refrigerated) for 2–3 days.

2. For the lentil-pistachio mix, add the pistachios, fennel seeds, cumin seeds and some salt and pepper to a small dry frying pan and cook over a high heat for 3–5 minutes until smelling fragrant. Tip into a bowl and allow to cool. Now roughly chop.

3. Into a small mixing bowl, add the chopped pistachio mix, the lentils, chopped mint, lemon zest, lemon juice and olive oil and toss well. This can also be refrigerated in a sealed container for 2–3 days now.

4. When you are ready to serve, spread the hummus onto a large plate (or four or six smaller ones) and top with the lentil-pistachio mix, a drizzle of extra virgin olive oil and mint leaves. Serve with your preferred pitta bread chunks and dip in.

Top Tip

This beetroot hummus is also delicious on its own, spread into sandwiches or on toast or as part of salad bowls.

Sweet Potato Falafel Wraps with Herby Tahini

Serves 4 (makes 12 falafel) | **Prep time:** 20 minutes + 10 minutes resting | **Cook time:** 20 minutes

Falafel and hummus are a match made in heaven, but these falafel have a little bit extra going for them, thanks to the addition of the antioxidant-rich sweet potato, plus the abundance of spices and herbs to pack in extra plant points. They are naturally gluten-free and high in fibre and protein, while the homemade herby tahini sauce is smooth, vibrant, creamy and full of healthy fats. These are great for filling wraps, tortillas or pitta breads and are the perfect feel-good food with some homemade hummus, pickles and greens. This is an ideal recipe for speedy lunches, midweek meals and picnics in the summertime.

For the sweet potato falafel

1 large sweet potato

1 spring onion, sliced

1 x 400g/14oz can chickpeas/
garbanzo beans, drained
and rinsed (240g/8½oz/1½
cups drained weight)

60g/2¼oz/½ cup chickpea
(gram) flour, sifted

35g/1¼oz/¼ cup
buckwheat flour

10g/¼oz/¼ packed cup
fresh coriander/cilantro

2 garlic cloves, peeled

1 tsp ground cumin

½ tsp ground coriander

½ tsp smoked paprika

a pinch of cayenne pepper

½ tsp baking powder

olive oil, for brushing

salt and pepper, to taste

For the herby tahini

3 tbsp runny smooth tahini

2 tbsp thick coconut yogurt

2 tbsp lemon juice

1 tbsp chopped fresh mint

1 tbsp chopped fresh
coriander/cilantro

1 garlic clove, peeled

½ tsp ground cumin

For the wraps

4 tbsp Homemade
Hummus (see page 159)

4 tortilla wraps or pitta
(gluten-free if needed)

4 handfuls of salad greens
(e.g. rocket/arugula,
watercress, baby spinach)

4 tbsp Pink Pickles
(see page 31)

80g/2¾oz/½ cup cherry
tomatoes, cut into quarters

4 tbsp pomegranate seeds

2 sprigs of fresh mint leaves

2 tbsp mixed sesame seeds

1. Start by making the sweet potato falafel. Stab the sweet potato all over with a knife and place on a plate. Microwave on High in 2-minute intervals, turning over each time, until soft to touch. This should take 5–6 minutes. Allow the sweet potato to cool for 5 minutes, then carefully remove the skin (you can eat this!) and mash the flesh, so you have 160g/5¾oz/⅔ cup of mashed sweet potato.

2. Add the sweet potato to a food processor or blender with all the other falafel ingredients, except the olive oil, and season with salt and pepper. Blend until mostly smooth, but some small chunks are okay. Leave the mix to rest for 10 minutes.

3. Preheat the oven to 200°C/400°F/Gas 6 and line a large baking sheet with baking parchment.

4. Divide the falafel mix into 12 golf ball-size pieces and roll into balls (wash your hands in between as they will be sticky). Place the balls on the lined baking sheet and brush or spray them with olive oil. Bake in the oven for 10 minutes, then turn the baking sheet around and bake for a further 5 minutes until crisping up and golden.

5. Meanwhile, make the herby tahini. Add all the ingredients to a small blender along with 1–2 tbsp water. Blend until smooth and pourable. Season with salt and pepper.

6. When ready to eat the falafel, spread some hummus onto the wraps or pittas (see Top Tips) and top with some salad greens, then add three falafel per wrap/pitta. Add on some pink pickles, cherry tomatoes, pomegranate seeds, mint leaves and sesame seeds.

7. These are best eaten straight away, or keep all the components separately. Refrigerate the falafel in a sealed container for 3–5 days, or freeze for 1 month, then defrost (if frozen) and eat cold. Refrigerate the herby tahini in a separate sealed container for 2–3 days.

Top Tips

If using pitta breads, you can also split them open and stuff everything inside, if you prefer! These falafel are also delicious in a salad; for example, on top of a Kale Caesar Salad with Crispy Tofu (see page 150) or Avocado, Strawberry and Chickpea Salad (see page 48).

Beany Mediterranean Orzo Salad

Serves 4 | **Prep time:** 15 minutes | **Cook time:** 20 minutes

Take your pasta salad lunch to the next level with this vibrant fibre- and protein-packed orzo salad loaded with gut-loving ingredients. The range of vegetables and legumes enrich the gut microbiome with added diversity, which is important for immune health and our mental health, as a surprising 90-95% of our serotonin is produced in the gut.

For the roasted vegetables

1 red pepper, deseeded and cut into small chunks

160g/5¾oz/1 cup cherry tomatoes, halved

½ tsp dried oregano

¼ tsp chilli flakes

½ tbsp olive oil

4 tbsp pine nuts

For the orzo salad

160g/5¾oz/1 cup dried orzo

2 x 400g/14oz cans beans of your choice (e.g. red kidney beans and chickpeas/ garbanzo beans), drained and rinsed (480g/1lb 1oz/3 cups drained weight)

160g/5¾oz/1 cup sun-dried tomatoes, chopped

160g/5¾oz/1 cup pitted green olives, sliced

2 spring onions/ scallions, thinly sliced

4 tbsp chopped fresh mixed herbs (e.g. basil, coriander/cilantro, chives)

For the dressing

2 tbsp extra virgin olive oil

1 tbsp lemon juice

1 tbsp balsamic vinegar

½ tbsp nutritional yeast

1 garlic clove, crushed

To serve

4 large handfuls of rocket/ arugula or baby spinach

1. Preheat the oven to 180°C/350°F/Gas 4 and line a baking sheet with baking parchment.

2. Start by roasting the vegetables. Add the red pepper, cherry tomatoes, oregano, chilli flakes, olive oil and some salt and pepper to the lined baking sheet and toss well. Bake in the oven for 20 minutes, turning the baking sheet around halfway through roasting. Add the pine nuts to a second small baking sheet and bake for the final 5 minutes of the cooking time, then allow to cool.

3. Meanwhile, cook the orzo for the salad according to the package directions (about 7–9 minutes), then drain and rinse under cold water.

4. While the orzo cooks, add the rest of the salad ingredients to a large bowl and stir together.

5. Make the dressing by whisking together all the ingredients in a small bowl with some salt and pepper to taste.

6. Into the salad bowl, add the cooled orzo, the roasted vegetables and the dressing. Toss well.

7. Divide the rocket or spinach between plates and top with the orzo salad. Sprinkle with the toasted pine nuts, and enjoy. This is also great with 4 tbsp of Tofu Feta (*see* page 32)

8. Eat straight away, or refrigerate leftovers in a sealed container for 2–3 days.

Top Tip
You can use any canned beans or legumes for this orzo salad; I also love cooked Puy lentils, butter/lima beans or black beans.

Sticky Tofu Halloumi Glow Bowls

Serves 4 | **Prep time:** 20 minutes + 20 minutes (or 1–2 hours) marinating | **Cook time:** 15 minutes

This may be my new favourite way to eat tofu as it's sticky, rich with salty Mediterranean flavours and slightly tangy. It's perfect for adding on top of this nutrient-dense salad of wholesome quinoa, a vibrant array of vegetables and fermented pickles and cabbage. The fermented foods boost good gut bacteria, which can support mood, while the almonds contain amino acids which contribute to the production of mood-boosting serotonin. Not only is this rainbow bowl pleasing to the eye, it's also loaded with different vitamins and minerals, plus avocado, which can help support the stress response.

Top Tip
Prep is key to make this recipe quick and easy. You can prep the hummus in advance (it's great for snacking) and marinate the tofu for a couple of hours ahead to let the flavours infuse.

For the salad

180g/6¼oz/1 cup quinoa

120g/4¼oz red
   cabbage, shredded

1 tsp apple cider vinegar

4 handfuls salad greens (e.g.
   watercress, rocket/arugula)

1 avocado, cut into quarters

1 small cucumber, cut
   into ½-moon slices

4 tbsp pomegranate seeds

4 tbsp Homemade Pink
   Pickles (see page 31)

2 sprigs of fresh mint leaves

For the tofu halloumi

2 x 200g/7oz blocks of
   extra-firm tofu, drained

2 tbsp olive oil

2 tbsp lemon juice

2 tbsp nutritional yeast

1 tsp dried oregano

1 tsp garlic granules

1 tsp salt

few grindings of black pepper

olive oil, for frying

16 stems of long-stem
   broccoli (approx.
   320g/11¼oz), trimmed

70g/2½oz/½ cup whole
   (skin on) almonds,
   roughly chopped

For the hot maple

2 tbsp maple syrup

½ tsp chilli flakes

For the homemade hummus

1 x 400g/14oz can chickpeas/
   garbanzo beans
   (240g/8½oz/1½ cups once
   drained, but keep the liquid)

2 tbsp extra virgin olive oil

2 tbsp runny smooth tahini

2 tbsp lemon juice

1 small garlic clove, peeled

1 tsp ground cumin

1. Start by preparing the tofu halloumi and marinade. Slice the tofu into 16 rectangles. In a large, shallow bowl, whisk together the olive oil, lemon juice, nutritional yeast, oregano, garlic granules, a pinch of salt and pepper until well mixed. Add in the tofu, turning the slices all over to coat evenly. Leave the tofu to marinate for 20 minutes (or cover and refrigerate for 1–2 hours, if you like).

2. Prepare the hot maple by stirring together the maple syrup and chilli flakes in a small bowl. Set aside.

3. While the tofu marinates, make the hummus. Drain the chickpeas, keeping the liquid from the can to one side. Add the chickpeas to a small blender or food processor with 60ml/2fl oz/¼ cup of the reserved liquid. Add in all the other ingredients and some salt and pepper, then blend together until really smooth and creamy, stopping to scrape down the sides as necessary. Transfer to a sealed container and refrigerate for 3–5 days (if making in advance).

4. Cook the quinoa according to the package directions, then set aside. For the quick pickled cabbage, add the cabbage to a bowl with the vinegar and salt and massage with your hands for 30 seconds to soften.

5. When the marinated tofu is ready, heat a large non-stick frying pan with a little olive oil and add in the tofu slices, ensuring they don't overlap (leave the marinade behind). Cook over a medium-high heat for 5 minutes until golden. Flip over and repeat until golden.

6. Pour half the hot maple over the tofu and allow it to sizzle and bubble. Flip all the tofu slices over to coat all sides with the glaze. Cook for a further 1–2 minutes, then carefully transfer to a plate. Now add the rest of the hot maple to the pan with the broccoli and almonds. Cook over a medium-high heat for 2–3 minutes, or until the broccoli is vibrant and the nuts are sticky. Remove both from the pan.

7. When ready to serve, divide the salad greens between four plates or bowls and top with the quinoa, the quick pickled cabbage, avocado, cucumber, some hummus and finally with the sticky tofu halloumi. Add some broccoli to each plate/bowl and sprinkle over the sticky almonds, then finish with the pomegranate seeds, pink pickles and mint leaves.

8. Enjoy straight away, or refrigerate in a sealed container for 2–3 days and enjoy cold.

CHAPTER 3

dinner

Cauliflower Gnocchi with Red Pepper Sauce

Serves 4 | **Prep time:** 25 minutes | **Cook time:** 40 minutes

This homemade cauliflower gnocchi is a revelation – it's just as comforting and nostalgic as potato-based gnocchi but with the added goodness of being made from cauliflower, buckwheat flour and oats. This naturally gluten-free and plant-based gnocchi is easy to make and is loaded with gut-loving fibre. The roasted red pepper sauce is rich, creamy and packed with Mediterranean flavours to transport you to Italy with every bite. The range of antioxidants in the fruits and vegetables add to the diversity, boosting your overall wellbeing.

Top Tip

Serve this cauliflower gnocchi with your favourite pasta sauces. Try it with the Green Goddess Pasta sauce (see page 80) or with the Lentil and Mushroom "Meatballs" with Homemade Tomato Sauce (see page 180).

For the cauliflower gnocchi

1 head of cauliflower, cut into florets (500g/1lb 2oz/5 cups florets)

140g/5oz/1 cup buckwheat flour, plus extra for dusting

100g/3½oz/1 cup oat flour

2 tbsp cornflour/cornstarch

salt and pepper, to taste

For the veg

1 tbsp olive oil

1 red onion, cut into small dice

4 garlic cloves, crushed

1 tsp dried oregano

1 tsp dried basil

½ tsp smoked paprika

400g/14oz/2½ cups cherry tomatoes, cut in half

100g/3½oz/4 cups curly kale (de-stemmed weight), shredded

4 sprigs of fresh basil, leaves only, shredded

2 tbsp lemon juice

For the roasted red pepper sauce

180g/6¼oz/1 cup roasted red peppers in oil (drained weight)

80g/2¾oz/½ cup sun-dried tomatoes

1 x 300g/10½oz block of silken tofu, drained (290g/10¼oz drained weight)

240ml/8½fl oz/1 cup plant-based milk

2 tbsp tomato purée/paste

2 tbsp lemon juice

2 tsp white miso paste

2 garlic cloves, peeled

To serve

4 tbsp Homemade Vegan Parmesan (see page 81)

2 sprigs of fresh basil

1. Start by preparing the gnocchi. Steam the cauliflower florets over a pan of simmering water until soft, about 10 minutes, then add to a food processor with all the other ingredients and season with salt and pepper. Process to a sticky dough texture, then scrape out onto a floured work surface. Knead for 1–2 minutes to make a smooth ball of dough, then divide into eight equal pieces.

2. Use your fingers to roll each piece into a sausage shape 10cm/4in long. Use a floured knife to cut each gnocchi length into 10 equal pieces. Flour a fork and press into each piece of gnocchi to make the classic grooves.

3. Bring a large pan of water to the boil, then add in a quarter of the gnocchi pieces. Cook in the bubbling water for 1–2 minutes until they rise to the surface, indicating they are cooked. Remove with a slotted spoon onto a plate and repeat to cook all the gnocchi. This can be prepared 2–3 days in advance, cooled and refrigerated in a sealed container, or frozen for 1 month (defrost if frozen), before continuing.

4. Meanwhile, heat a large non-stick frying pan with the olive oil and fry off the onion, garlic, dried herbs and paprika over a medium-high heat for 5 minutes, stirring often. Now add in the tomatoes with some salt and pepper, then cover and cook over a medium heat for 10 minutes, stirring occasionally.

5. While the tomato mixture simmers, add all the ingredients for the roasted red pepper sauce to a blender and blend until smooth.

6. Pour the cooked gnocchi and the roasted red pepper sauce into the veg in the frying pan, cover and warm through over a medium heat for 5 minutes.

7. Add the kale and basil to the pan with the lemon juice. Cook for 5 more minutes until the kale has wilted.

8. Ladle the gnocchi and sauce into four bowls and top with some vegan parmesan and fresh basil leaves.

9. Enjoy straight away, or cool, then refrigerate the combined gnocchi and sauce in a sealed container for 2–3 days, or freeze for 1 month, then defrost (if frozen) before warming back up in a pan.

One-pan Courgette Lasagne

Serves 4 | **Prep time:** 15 minutes | **Cook time:** 35 minutes

Growing up half-Italian, lasagne brings back so many fond memories for me, and so I wanted to recreate a plant-based, more wholesome and easier version. This one-pan creation doesn't require an oven to cook the lasagne, all the work is done in a large frying pan, and the flavours are amazing. It is packed with antioxidant-rich vegetables, herbs and tomatoes which support a healthy gut and in turn our gut–brain axis. Top this pasta pan with some of my No Nuts Homemade Cream Cheese (a source of tofu which boosts good gut bacteria) and homemade Sun-dried Tomato Pesto (full of gut-loving unsaturated fats and serotonin-producing amino acids) – see my recipes on pages 198 and 195 – for the best meal to share with loved ones.

For the lasagne

1 tbsp olive oil

1 red onion, cut into small dice

4 garlic cloves, crushed

1 red pepper, deseeded and cut into small dice

1 tsp dried oregano

1 tsp dried basil

2 courgettes/zucchini, thinly sliced or ribboned

2 x 400g/14oz cans chopped tomatoes

2 tbsp tomato purée/paste

1 x 400g/14oz can brown or green lentils, drained and rinsed (240g/8½oz/1½ cups drained weight)

480ml/17fl oz/2 cups vegetable stock

240g/8½oz dried lasagne sheets, broken up

salt and pepper, to taste

To serve

8 heaped tbsp No Nuts Homemade Cream Cheese (see page 198)

4 tbsp Sun-dried Tomato Pesto (see page 195)

2 tbsp Homemade Vegan Parmesan (see page 81)

1. Heat a large non-stick frying pan with the olive oil, and once hot, add the onion, garlic and red pepper with a pinch of salt. Fry off over a high heat for 5 minutes until softening, then add in the dried herbs and some black pepper. Fry for 1 minute until fragrant.

2. Now add in the courgettes, chopped tomatoes, tomato purée, lentils, stock and broken-up lasagne sheets, stirring well so that they are all mixed together evenly.

3. Place a lid on the pan and allow to bubble away over a medium heat for 25 minutes, stirring occasionally, so that the pasta all cooks evenly. The lasagne is ready when the pasta is al dente and the tomato sauce is bubbly and thickened.

4. Remove the lid, spoon over the cream cheese and top with the sun-dried tomato pesto and vegan parmesan. You can add fresh basil leaves, if you like.

5. Portion into four bowls and enjoy warm.

6. Once cool, you can refrigerate the lasagne in a sealed container (ideally without the toppings) for 2–3 days, or freeze for 1 month, then defrost (if frozen) and warm back up in a frying pan before serving with the toppings.

Top Tip

Stir the mixture well and break apart any pieces of pasta that stick together during cooking, otherwise they won't cook evenly. Use gluten-free lasagne sheets where needed.

Golden Miso Curry Noodle Bowls

Serves 4 | **Prep time:** 15 minutes | **Cook time:** 30 minutes

Curry and noodles together are my form of comfort food, ideal for creating these cosy, feel-good bowls that you'll come back to time and again. This mind-fuelling noodle recipe is similar to a creamy ramen and packs in loads of gut-friendly ingredients like antioxidant-rich spices, miso paste, coconut milk and tofu, while the vibrant garnishes and dark leafy greens contain magnesium, which can help to support good mood.

For the miso curry sauce

1 small butternut squash, peeled, deseeded and chopped (approx. 600g/1lb 5oz/4 cups once prepped)

1 large carrot, washed and chopped into cubes

1 tsp smoked paprika

1 tsp ground cumin

1 tsp ground turmeric

½ tsp ground coriander

a thumb-size piece of root ginger, peeled and grated

3 tbsp olive oil

4 garlic cloves, left whole

1 tbsp brown rice miso paste

1 x 400ml/14fl oz can full-fat or light coconut milk

120ml/4fl oz/½ cup water

juice of 1 lime

salt and pepper, to taste

For the tofu and broccoli

1 tbsp sesame oil

2 x 200g/7oz blocks of extra-firm tofu, drained and cut into small chunks/squares

16 stems of long-stem broccoli (approx. 320g/11¼oz), trimmed

2 tbsp tamari soy sauce

2 tbsp maple syrup

4 tbsp mixed white and black sesame seeds

For the bowls

4 nests of dried noodles of your choice (e.g. udon, buckwheat or ramen)

1 red chilli, thinly sliced

4 tsp thick coconut yogurt

4 tsp chilli oil

2 sprigs of fresh coriander/cilantro, leaves only

2 tbsp mixed white and black sesame seeds

1. Start by preparing the curry sauce. Preheat the oven to 200°C/400°F/Gas 6 and line a large baking sheet with baking parchment.

2. Add the butternut squash to the lined baking sheet with the carrot. In a small bowl, stir together the paprika, cumin, turmeric, ground coriander, ginger, olive oil and some salt and pepper to make a paste. Spoon this all over the vegetables and toss well. Nestle in the garlic cloves, then bake in the oven for 25 minutes until the vegetables are tender, stirring halfway through.

3. When the vegetables have 10 minutes left, prepare the tofu and broccoli. Heat the sesame oil in a large saucepan and add the tofu. Cook over a medium-high heat for 8–10 minutes until golden on all sides. Now add the broccoli and cook for another 2–3 minutes until the broccoli is vibrant in colour. Pour over the tamari, maple syrup and sesame seeds and toss quickly to coat everything with the glaze. Remove from the heat and set aside in the pan to keep warm.

4. Meanwhile, cook the noodles according to the package directions, then drain and rinse under cold water to stop them from overcooking.

5. When the vegetables are cooked, remove the garlic cloves and pour all of the vegetables (and any extra oils) into a blender. Squeeze the garlic out from their skins into the blender, then add the miso paste, coconut milk, water and lime juice. Carefully blend until really smooth and creamy. Pour into a large saucepan and warm through over a low heat.

6. To serve, divide the curry sauce between four bowls and add in the noodles. Top with the sticky tofu and broccoli and garnish with the chilli slices, swirls of coconut yogurt and chilli oil, coriander leaves and extra sesame seeds.

7. Enjoy straight away. To keep for later, once cool, refrigerate the curry sauce and the tofu/broccoli mix in two separate containers for 2–3 days, then warm back up before serving. Or, freeze the curry sauce for 1 month, then defrost before heating back up.

Top Tip

You can add other vegetables to the roasting mix, like pumpkin or sweet potato instead of the butternut squash, or deseeded red pepper instead of the carrot.

Roasted Cauliflower Nuggets with Tzatziki

Serves 4 as a starter or small plate | **Prep time:** 25 minutes | **Cook time:** 40 minutes

These spicy, sticky and delicious cauliflower nuggets have so much flavour, colour and texture and are a fantastic vegetable-based alternative to regular nuggets. They are even better served with a gut-healthy and refreshing tzatziki dip made with coconut yogurt, a fermented food that supports gut bacteria, lime juice and antioxidant-rich spices. These nuggets are also baked, not fried, and contain oat and buckwheat flour in the batter, both of which are high in fibre and great for gradually releasing sugar into the bloodstream. They are fun to make and eat (with sticky fingers!) and perfect for sharing – the ultimate feel-good food.

Top Tip
These are delicious served with some pitta breads or alongside the Sweet Potato Falafel (see page 154).

For the cauliflower and batter

1 medium cauliflower,
  leaves and florets

50g/1¾oz/½ cup oat flour

70g/2½oz/½ cup
  buckwheat flour

1 tsp garlic granules

1 tsp onion powder

1 tsp smoked paprika

1 tbsp nutritional yeast

240ml/8½fl oz/1 cup
  plant-based milk

olive or avocado oil, for
  spraying/brushing

salt and pepper, to taste

For the gochujang sauce

1½ tbsp gochujang paste

1½ tbsp tomato purée/paste

1½ tbsp tamari soy sauce

1½ tbsp maple syrup

1 tsp white miso paste

juice of 1 lime

For the tzatziki

1 small cucumber
  (approx. 120g/4¼oz)

120g/4¼oz/½ cup thick
  coconut yogurt

1 tbsp chopped fresh mint

1 tbsp chopped fresh chives

juice of 1 lime

¼ tsp ground cumin

½ tsp cayenne pepper

To serve

2 sprigs of fresh mint,
  leaves only

1 tbsp mixed white and
  black sesame seeds

1. Preheat the oven to 200°C/400°F/Gas 6 and line two large baking sheets with baking parchment.

2. Tear off the outer leaves of the cauliflower and leave to one side. Now break up all the cauliflower into florets – you'll have about 600g/1lb 5oz/4 heaped cups of florets.

3. In a large mixing bowl, whisk together the flours, garlic granules, onion powder, paprika, nutritional yeast, milk and salt and pepper. Add in the cauliflower florets and toss well.

4. Use a fork or tongs to place the cauliflower florets on one lined baking sheet, leaving the excess batter in the bowl. Brush or spray the florets with olive or avocado oil, then bake for 25 minutes, carefully turning after 15 minutes.

5. Add the cauliflower leaves to the batter bowl and toss well, then pick them from the bowl, allow the excess batter to drip off and place on the second lined baking sheet (discard any leftover batter). Spray or brush with oil and bake for the final 10 minutes.

6. Meanwhile, in a second large, heatproof bowl, whisk together all the gochujang sauce ingredients with some salt and pepper.

7. When the cauliflower florets and leaves are ready, place them in the gochujang bowl and toss well. Pick out the florets and place back on the baking sheet, then bake in the oven for 10–15 minutes, until sticky and starting to char. Do the same with the leaves, baking them for 5–10 minutes.

8. While they bake, grate the cucumber for the tzatziki and leave it to sit in a sieve/fine-mesh strainer over a bowl for 5 minutes. Now squeeze out the excess water until the cucumber reduces by half (you can drink the juice!).

9. Break the cucumber apart into a medium bowl, then add in the rest of the tzatziki ingredients with some salt and pepper and stir well.

10. Serve the roasted cauliflower nuggets (florets and leaves) warm with the bowl of tzatziki, with the mint leaves and sesame seeds sprinkled over.

11. Refrigerate leftover cold cauliflower nuggets and tzatziki in separate containers for 2–3 days and eat cold, or warm up the nuggets in a preheated oven at 200°C/400°F/Gas 6 for 10 minutes (florets) or 5 minutes (leaves).

Mushroom, Bean and Lentil Chilli

Serves 4 as a main; serves 6 as a smaller portion | **Prep time:** 15 minutes | **Cook time:** 30 minutes

Nothing beats a warming bowl of chilli non-carne and this recipe is packed with extra vegetables, spices and "meaty" mushrooms. The secret to a rich and delicious sauce is adding dark/bittersweet chocolate, which is a natural mood booster thanks to the abundance of flavonoids it contains, so choose a high-quality dark chocolate where you can. The mix of beans and lentils adds a variety of fibre and plants, all of which feed the gut to improve our everyday health.

For the chilli

1 tbsp olive oil

225g/8oz/3 cups
  mushrooms, finely chopped

1 red onion, finely diced

1 red pepper, deseeded
  and finely diced

3 garlic cloves, crushed

1 tsp hot smoked paprika

1 tsp ground cumin

½ tsp ground coriander

½ tsp ground cinnamon

1 tbsp balsamic or
  red wine vinegar

1 x 400g/14oz can red
  kidney beans, drained
  and rinsed (240g/8½oz/1½
  cups drained weight)

1 x 240g/8½oz pouch (1½
  cups) cooked lentils (e.g.
  Puy or green lentils)

1 x 400g/14oz can
  chopped tomatoes

2 tbsp tomato purée/paste

80ml/2¾floz/1/3 cup water

14g/½oz dark/bittersweet
  chocolate, chopped

salt and pepper, to taste

For the guacamole

1 large ripe avocado

1 tbsp lemon juice

1 spring onion/scallion,
  finely chopped

1 tbsp chopped fresh herbs
  (e.g. coriander/cilantro,
  parsley or chives)

To serve

4–6 servings of cooked
  brown rice (or other
  whole grain)

4 tbsp thick coconut yogurt

2 handfuls of baked
  tortilla chips

a few sprigs of fresh
  coriander/cilantro
  or parsley

1. For the chilli, heat the olive oil in a large non-stick frying pan, and once hot, add the mushrooms with a pinch of salt. Fry over a medium-high heat for 5 minutes to release all their juices and cook down.

2. Add the onion, red pepper and garlic and cook for 5 more minutes until softened.

3. Add all the ground spices with some black pepper and fry off for 1 minute until smelling fragrant. Pour over the vinegar to deglaze the pan and absorb all the spices.

4. Now add the beans, lentils, tomatoes, tomato purée, water and dark chocolate. Stir well and bring to a gentle bubble, then cook with a lid on for 10–15 minutes until really thick and glossy, stirring a few times so that the beans don't stick.

5. For the guacamole, scoop out the flesh from the avocado and place in a small bowl with the other ingredients, then mash with a fork, until mostly smooth with some chunks for texture. Season to taste with salt and pepper.

6. To serve the chilli, divide the cooked rice (or whole grain) between bowls and top with the warm chilli. Add on the coconut yogurt, guacamole, tortilla chips and herb sprigs.

7. For any leftovers, cool the chilli, then refrigerate in a sealed container for 2–3 days, or freeze for 1 month, then defrost (if frozen) and warm back up to eat. Refrigerate leftover guacamole in a separate sealed container for 1–2 days.

Top Tip
You can use any beans for this recipe, variety is key. Black beans or a can of mixed beans would be delicious, too.

Sweet Potato Pizzas

Serves 4 | **Prep time:** 20 minutes + 5 minutes cooling | **Cook time:** 25 minutes

Pizza is one of life's little pleasures and these pizza bases can be enjoyed by everyone, as they are made with wholesome, plant-based, gluten-free ingredients. They are naturally high in antioxidants from the sweet potato, while the buckwheat and chickpea (gram) flour add fibre and protein. These are the ultimate mood-boosting pizzas, and you can get as creative as you like or follow this recipe for crispy chickpea/garbanzo bean, tomato and olive pizzas. Make the bases, lay out your toppings and allow everyone to pick and choose.

Top Tip

You can use this base for any number of toppings! Make the bases up to the end of step 6 and then get creative: try adding any roasted veg, caramelized onions, baked tofu, canned beans, or classic tomato sauce, fresh basil and some vegan cheese, and bake for 5–10 minutes.

For the pizza bases

2 large sweet potatoes

2 tbsp ground flaxseed

4 tbsp water

140g/5oz/1 cup buckwheat flour, plus extra for dusting

4 tbsp chickpea (gram) flour, sifted

2 tbsp cornflour/cornstarch

2 tbsp hulled hemp seeds

2 tsp baking powder

1 tbsp olive oil

salt and pepper, to taste

For the toppings

1 x 400g/14oz can chickpeas/garbanzo beans, drained, rinsed and patted dry (240g/8½oz/1½ cups drained weight)

½ tsp hot smoked paprika

½ tsp dried oregano

1 tbsp olive oil

8 tbsp Sun-dried Tomato Pesto (see page 195, or use shop-bought)

2 spring onions/ scallions, sliced

160g/5¾oz/1 cup cherry tomatoes, cut in half or into quarters

160g/5¾oz/1 cup pitted green or black olives, sliced

4 large handfuls of salad leaves (e.g. watercress, lettuce and/or spinach)

4 tbsp Homemade Pink Pickles (see page 31)

1 quantity of Tahini Sauce (see page 72)

4 tbsp mixed seeds

1. Stab the sweet potatoes all over with a knife. Microwave on High for 2-minute intervals, flipping them over each time, until soft (about 6 minutes). Allow the sweet potatoes to cool for 5 minutes, peel away the skin (you can eat it!) and mash the flesh. You should have 320g/11¼oz/2 cups of mash.

2. Preheat the oven to 200°C/400°F/Gas 6 and line two large baking sheets (or four small ones) with baking parchment.

3. Stir together the ground flaxseed and water in a small bowl and leave for 5 minutes to form a gel.

4. For the pizza dough, add the sweet potato mash to a large mixing bowl with the flaxseed gel, buckwheat flour, chickpea flour, cornflour, hemp seeds, baking powder and salt and pepper. Stir with a spoon to a shaggy dough, then tip onto a floured work surface. Bring together into a small ball of dough, kneading gently for 1–2 minutes. Divide the dough into four equal pieces and roll these into balls.

5. Lightly flour the baking parchment on the baking sheets and place a ball of dough on top (one or two per sheet, depending on the size). Lightly flour the surface of the dough and roll out each ball to a circle 20cm/8in diameter. Brush off the excess flour and brush with the olive oil. Bake in the oven for 10 minutes, turning the baking sheets around halfway through.

7. Meanwhile, line another baking sheet with baking parchment. Add the chickpeas to this with the paprika, oregano, olive oil and salt and pepper. Toss well, then bake for 20 minutes, at the same time as the pizza bases.

8. Remove the pizza bases from the oven, then spread some pesto over each one and top with the spring onions, half the tomatoes and half the olives. Return to the oven for 5–10 minutes more, until crisping at the edges.

9. Use a large spatula to carefully remove the pizza bases and plate them up. Top with the salad leaves, the remaining tomatoes and olives and the crispy chickpeas. Serve with the pink pickles, tahini sauce and seeds.

11. Enjoy straight away, or later the same day (refrigerate once cool). Alternatively, prepare the pizza bases up to the end of step 6 and remove after the initial bake. Cool, wrap in cling film/plastic wrap and refrigerate for 2–3 days, or freeze for 1 month, then defrost (if frozen) before topping with the pesto and continuing to bake the pizzas as above.

Spinach and Tofu Curry with Coconut Rice

Serves 4 | **Prep time:** 15 minutes | **Cook time:** 25 minutes

Friday night "fakeaways" just got a lot better with this delicious simple yet vibrant curry that everyone will love. It's even better served with homemade cucumber raita, some coconutty brown rice and crispy tofu. The base of the sauce is loaded with antioxidant-rich spices, dark leafy spinach and juicy tomatoes, which blend into the creamiest super-green curry sauce. The abundance of vegetables in this meal will support your brain and your gut, while the tofu and pink pickles are great for feeding your gut. Serve with flatbreads, naan breads or pitta breads and Homemade Pink Pickles (see page 31).

Top Tip
You can add any vegetables to the tofu as it cooks, like broccoli florets instead of green beans, or diced aubergine/ eggplant instead of red pepper.

For the coconut rice

300g/10½oz/1½ cups short-
   grain brown rice, rinsed

1 x 400ml/14floz can light
   or full-fat coconut milk

For the curry

1 tbsp olive oil

1 white onion, finely chopped

4 garlic cloves, crushed

a large thumb-size piece of
   ginger, peeled and grated

1 tsp garam masala

1 tsp ground cumin

½ tsp ground turmeric

½ tsp smoked paprika

1 beefsteak tomato
   (160g/5¾oz), finely chopped

150g/5½oz/5 cups spinach

1 x 400ml/14fl oz can light
   or full-fat coconut milk

juice of 1 lime

1 tbsp tamari soy sauce

salt and pepper, to taste

For the tofu and vegetables

1 tbsp olive oil

2 x 200g/7oz blocks
   extra-firm tofu, cubed

1 red pepper, deseeded
   and sliced into strips

200g/7oz green
   beans, halved

For the raita

1 small cucumber

120g/4¼oz/½ cup thick
   coconut yogurt

1 tbsp chopped fresh mint

1 tbsp chopped fresh
   coriander/cilantro,
   plus extra to serve

juice of 1 lime

¼ tsp ground cumin

a pinch of cayenne pepper

To serve

1 red chilli, sliced (optional)

1. Start by making the coconut rice. Add the rice to a medium saucepan with the coconut milk, 240ml/8½fl oz/1 cup water and a pinch of salt. Cover and bring to the boil, then reduce the heat to low-medium and cook for 20 minutes without stirring. Now remove the lid and cook for 5 more minutes until all the liquid has been absorbed, then stir at the end.

2. Meanwhile, make the curry sauce. Add the olive oil to a large non-stick pan with the onion, garlic and ginger. Fry off over a high heat for 5 minutes to soften the onion, then add the ground spices and fry for 1 minute until fragrant. Add the tomato and spinach, season with salt and pepper and cook while stirring for a few minutes until the spinach has wilted and is darker in colour.

3. Transfer the spinach mix to a large blender with the coconut milk, lime juice and tamari and blend until really smooth. Pour into a medium saucepan and keep warm over a low heat.

4. Using the same frying pan as before, cook the tofu and veg. Add the olive oil to the pan, and once hot, add the tofu, red pepper and green beans. Cook over a high heat for 5–8 minutes, tossing regularly, until the tofu is golden and the vegetables are cooked through.

5. Finally, prepare the raita. Grate the cucumber and squeeze out all the excess water using your hands (you can drink the cucumber water!), then break apart into a small bowl. Stir in the rest of the ingredients and season with salt and pepper.

6. To serve, divide the green curry sauce between four bowls. Spoon in some coconut rice and top with the tofu and vegetables. Add on some raita and serve with your favourite flatbreads, coriander, pink pickles and the chilli slices (if using).

7. Enjoy straight away, or you can refrigerate the leftover curry sauce with the tofu and vegetables in a sealed container for 2–3 days, or freeze for 1 month, then defrost (if frozen) and warm back up in a pan. Refrigerate the raita in a separate sealed container for 2–3 days, and refrigerate the rice in another sealed container for 1 day, then enjoy cold or heat up in a pan with a splash of water until piping hot.

Sticky Miso Mushrooms and Aubergines with Creamy Butter Beans

Serves 4 | **Prep time:** 20 minutes | **Cook time:** 25 minutes

This is my favourite kind of food. It's nourishing, comforting and packed with flavour and texture – and it makes me so happy to eat it. The aubergines/eggplants are glazed and sticky, while the beans are saucy and loaded with fibre and protein. The dark leafy spinach and vegetables have a prebiotic effect in the body, feeding our microbiome.

Top Tip
For a more filling meal,
enjoy these beans with
cooked brown rice or
some flatbreads.

For the creamy sauce

1 x 400g/14oz can butter/lima
beans (240g/8½oz/1½ cups
drained), keep the liquid

60g/2¼oz/¼ cup thick
coconut yogurt

60ml/2floz/¼ cup
plant-based milk

3 tbsp runny smooth tahini

2 tbsp hulled hemp seeds

1 tbsp lemon juice

1 tbsp tamari soy sauce

For the beans

1 tbsp olive oil

1 leek or 2 large spring
onions/scallions, thinly sliced

3 garlic cloves, crushed

½ red chilli, finely chopped
(optional), plus extra
to serve (optional)

1 x 400g/14oz can
butter/lima beans,
drained and rinsed

90g/3¼oz/3 cups spinach

For the mushrooms/aubergines

2 tbsp tamari soy sauce

2 tbsp maple syrup

2 tsp brown rice miso paste

juice of 2 limes

2 small spring onions/
scallions, thinly sliced

4 garlic cloves, crushed

a thumb-size piece of root
ginger, peeled and grated

2 tbsp olive oil

1 large aubergine/eggplant,
sliced into rounds

400g/14oz/4 heaped cups
mushrooms, quartered

To serve

1 quantity of Tahini
Sauce (see page 72)

handful of fresh coriander/
cilantro, parsley or mint

2 tbsp sesame seeds

1. Start by making the creamy sauce for the beans. Drain the butter beans, keeping 120ml/4fl oz/½ cup of the liquid. Add the beans, reserved bean liquid and the rest of the sauce ingredients, plus salt and pepper to taste, to a blender and blend until smooth. Set aside.

2. Now prepare the beans. Heat a non-stick pan with the olive oil, and once hot, add the leek or spring onions, garlic and chilli with some salt and pepper. Fry over a medium-high heat for 5 minutes to soften the leek/onion before adding in the creamy sauce and butter beans. Stir well, cover and warm through over a medium heat for 5 minutes. Now add in the spinach, stir well and cook for 5 more minutes to wilt the spinach.

3. Meanwhile, for the mushrooms and aubergines, make the marinade by stirring together the tamari, maple syrup, miso paste, lime juice and 4 tbsp water until smooth. Add the spring onions, garlic and ginger and season to taste.

4. Add 1 tbsp of the olive oil to a large non-stick pan and fry off the aubergine slices (working in batches) over a high heat for 5–7 minutes to soften. Flip over and cook the second side, then remove from the pan. Add the remaining olive oil and the mushrooms to the pan and fry over a high heat for 5 minutes, so the mushrooms are glossy and they release their juices. Return the aubergine slices to the pan and add the marinade. Allow to bubble and turn sticky for about 5 minutes, tossing the vegetables to evenly coat them.

5. To serve, scoop the creamy beans into four bowls and top each portion with a few slices of aubergine and some mushrooms. Drizzle over any extra marinade. Top with the tahini sauce, chilli slices (if using) herbs and sesame seeds.

6. Enjoy straight away, or allow the creamy beans and vegetables to cool, then refrigerate in separate sealed containers for 2–3 days. Warm back up in a pan as needed.

Black Bean Mango Salsa Taco Bowls

Serves 4 | **Prep time:** 20 minutes + cooling | **Cook time:** 10 minutes

This vibrant and zesty salsa bowl recipe is quick and easy to make and is great for when the temperature outside heats up. The salsa is fresh, fruity and rich in protein, plus all the different fruits and vegetables are great for adding diversity to your gut microbiome. The taco shells are crunchy and crispy and can be made with your favourite tortilla wraps. This meal is great to share with friends and family and it will transport you straight to summer.

For the bowls

4 large soft flour tortilla wraps (gluten-free where needed)

1 tbsp olive oil

For the salsa

1 large ripe mango, peeled, pitted and cubed

1 x 400g/14oz can black beans, drained and rinsed (240g/8½oz/1½ cups drained weight)

1 x 198g/7oz can sweetcorn kernels, drained (160g/5¾oz/1 cup drained weight)

160g/5¾oz/1 cup cherry tomatoes, cut into quarters

80g/2¾oz/½ cup pomegranate seeds

2 spring onions/ scallions, sliced

2 tbsp chopped fresh mixed herbs (e.g. coriander/ cilantro, mint and chives)

1 red chilli, finely chopped (optional)

For the dressing

1 tbsp olive oil

juice of 1 lime

1 tsp maple syrup

1 tsp apple cider vinegar

¼ tsp ground cumin

¼ tsp hot smoked paprika

salt and pepper, to taste

To serve

1 Little Gem lettuce, chopped

2 large handfuls of rocket/arugula

2 ripe avocados, sliced

4 tbsp Homemade Pink Pickles (see page 31)

4 tbsp mixed seeds

1 quantity of Herby Tahini (see page 155)

1. Preheat the oven to 180°C/350°F/Gas 4 and have four 20cm/8in round deep cake pans or deep ovenproof dishes to hand.

2. Brush the tortilla wraps with the olive oil on both sides, then nestle, mould or pinch them into the cake pans or dishes to make bowl shapes (if you only have two suitable cake pans/dishes, just make two bowls at a time, then repeat to make the other two). Bake in the oven for 10 minutes until crisp. Remove from the oven, then remove from the cake pans/dishes and allow to cool on a wire/ cooling rack.

3. To make the salsa, add all the ingredients to a bowl and toss together.

4. Make the dressing by whisking together all the ingredients in a small bowl, then pour it over the salsa. Toss again.

5. Fill the tortilla taco bowls with some lettuce and rocket and top with the salsa. Add on some avocado slices, pink pickles, mixed seeds and a good drizzle of herby tahini.

6. Once the taco bowls are filled, eat straight away. You can refrigerate the combined salsa and dressing in a sealed container for 2–3 days, but the tortilla taco bowls are best eaten freshly made.

Top Tip

Try this salsa with some cooked whole grains like quinoa or buckwheat, or rolled into a tortilla wrap for a fun spin on this meal.

Lentil and Mushroom "Meatballs"
with Homemade Tomato Sauce

Serves 4 | **Prep time:** 20 minutes + 10 minutes resting | **Cook time:** 30 minutes

I have such fond memories of eating fresh tomato sauce and pasta with my family, and this plant-based, high-protein and high-fibre recipe is just as nostalgic. This is a wonderful one to make for special occasions or dinner parties and you can prep it all ahead of time. The meatballs contain lentils and mushrooms which create a "meaty" texture, with both of these also containing prebiotic fibre to nourish the gut, while the walnuts contain tryptophan, an amino acid responsible for producing mood-boosting serotonin.

For the lentil meatballs

200g/7oz mushrooms, such
    as closed cup or chestnut

1 tbsp olive oil, plus extra
    for brushing/spraying

1 onion, cut into small dice

3 garlic cloves, crushed

1 red pepper, deseeded
    and cut into small dice

1 tsp smoked paprika

1 tsp ground cumin

1 tsp dried mixed herbs

1 x 240g/8½oz pouch (1½
    cups) cooked Puy lentils

70g/2½oz/2/3 cup walnuts

25g/1oz/¼ cup rolled oats

2 tbsp nutritional yeast

2 tbsp ground flaxseed
    or chia seeds

2 tbsp tomato purée/paste

1 tbsp brown rice miso paste

3 sprigs of fresh basil

salt and pepper, to taste

For the tomato sauce

1 tbsp olive oil

1 onion, cut into small dice

2 garlic cloves, crushed

½ tsp dried mixed herbs

1 x 400g/14oz can
    chopped tomatoes

160g/5¾oz/2/3 cup tomato
    passata/sieved tomatoes

120ml/4fl oz/½ cup
    vegetable stock

2 tbsp tomato purée/paste

1 tsp light soft brown sugar

To serve

4 servings of your favourite
    pasta, cooked and drained

4 tbsp Homemade Vegan
    Parmesan (see page 81)

a large sprig of fresh
    basil, leaves only

1. Start by making the lentil meatballs. Add the mushrooms to a food processor and blitz until really small. Heat a large non-stick frying pan with the olive oil, and once hot, add the mushrooms with a pinch of salt. Cook over a medium-high heat for 5 minutes, allowing the mushrooms to release their juices. Now add in the onion, garlic, red pepper, paprika, cumin and dried herbs. Season with pepper and continue to fry off for 10 minutes, to soften the vegetables.

2. Pour the mushroom mix back into the food processor and add all the remaining ingredients. Pulse the mix until it becomes sticky and holds together well. You want to remove any big lumps. Allow the mix to rest for 10 minutes.

3. Meanwhile, preheat the oven to 180°C/350°F/Gas 4 and line a large baking sheet with baking parchment.

4. Divide and roll the meatball mix into 20 balls, each about the size of a golf ball, and place on the lined baking sheet. Brush (or spray) with olive oil and bake in the oven for 15 minutes, turning the baking sheet around halfway through cooking. The balls will darken in colour and feel crispy on the outside. Cool for 5 minutes on the baking sheet before moving them to serve.

5. Meanwhile, make the tomato sauce. Using the same pan as above, heat the olive oil and add the onion and garlic. Fry over a medium-high heat for 5 minutes, then add the dried herbs and fry for 1 minute. Pour in the rest of the ingredients and season with salt and pepper. Stir well, bring to a gentle bubble and cover with a lid. Simmer over a medium heat for 10 minutes.

6. To serve, stir the cooked pasta through the tomato sauce, then divide between four plates or bowls. Top with the lentil meatballs, some vegan parmesan and basil leaves. Enjoy straight away.

7. You can make the tomato sauce and meatballs ahead of time and refrigerate them separately in sealed containers for 2–3 days, or freeze for 1 month, then defrost (if frozen) and warm back up to eat.

Happy Mind

Dinner

Top Tip
These "meatballs" are also great in a sandwich with the tomato sauce (hot or cold). or in pitta breads like in my Sweet Potato Falafel recipe on page 154.

CHAPTER 4

snacks
& dessert

Raspberry Ripple Layer Cake

Serves 10–12 | **Prep time:** 30 minutes + cooling | **Cook time:** 30 minutes

Raspberries and lemon go together perfectly in this summery showstopper cake. It's naturally egg-free, dairy-free and easily gluten-free and is loaded with feel-good ingredients like homemade raspberry chia seed jam (full of omega-3 fatty acids), coconut yogurt and oat flour, too. The gut-healthy ingredients help to support the gut–brain axis, important for overall wellbeing, while the fresh berries contain flavonoids which can support the brain and mood balance. Plus, this cake just makes you smile, so enjoy! I like to prepare the cake sponges the day before serving to make life easier. Wrap the cooled cakes in cling film (or stack on a plate and cover) and keep refrigerated.

For the raspberry jam
240g/8½oz/2 cups fresh raspberries
grated zest of 1 lemon
1 tbsp lemon juice
1 tbsp coconut sugar
1 tbsp chia seeds

For the sponge cakes
360ml/12½fl oz/1½ cups plant-based milk
½ tbsp apple cider vinegar
188g/6½oz/1¼ cups coconut sugar
grated zest of 1 lemon
90g/3¼oz/⅜ cup thick coconut yogurt
90ml/3¼fl oz/⅜ cup light olive oil
1½ tbsp chia seeds
1 tsp vanilla extract
315g/11oz/2¼ cups self-raising/self-rising flour*
75g/2¾oz/¾ cup oat flour
1 tsp baking powder
½ tsp bicarbonate of soda/baking soda
a pinch of salt

1. Start by making the raspberry jam as this will need to cool down slightly. Add the raspberries, lemon zest, lemon juice and coconut sugar to a medium saucepan and bring to the boil over a high heat. Continue to bubble for 5 minutes, stirring well to break down the berries. Once the berries are glossy and sticky, add the chia seeds, then remove from the heat. Stir well and allow to cool for 20 minutes to thicken.

2. Preheat the oven to 180°C/350°F/Gas 4. Grease and line the bases of three 15cm/6in shallow round sandwich cake pans with baking parchment.

3. Stir together the milk and vinegar in a jug and leave to curdle for 5 minutes.

4. In a large mixing bowl, rub the coconut sugar and lemon zest together for a few seconds with your fingers, to bring out the lemon flavours. Pour in the milk-vinegar mix, the yogurt, olive oil, chia seeds and vanilla. Whisk until combined.

5. Sift in the self-raising flour, then add all the remaining ingredients. Whisk to a smooth cake batter, being careful not to over-mix.

6. Divide the batter equally between the three lined cake pans (scales are easiest for this) and smooth over the tops. Spoon 3–4 tsp of the raspberry jam onto each cake and lightly swirl through. Save the leftover jam for the cake filling (it will keep refrigerated in a sealed container for 3–5 days).

7. Bake the cakes in the oven for 30 minutes until well-risen, golden on top and an inserted skewer comes out clean.

For the frosting

240g/8½oz/1 cup thick coconut yogurt

3 tbsp vegan cream cheese

3 tbsp vegan vanilla protein powder

3 tbsp freeze-dried raspberry powder

1 tbsp plant-based milk, if needed

To decorate

60g/2¼oz/½ cup fresh raspberries

1 tbsp crushed pistachios

Top Tip

*If making this cake gluten-free, use your preferred gluten-free flour (and if it doesn't contain xanthan gum, add ½ tsp of xanthan gum to your flour blend), and use gluten-free baking powder.

8. Leave the cakes to rest in the cake pans for 10 minutes, then carefully lift out and leave to cool fully on a wire/cooling rack. Once cool, carefully slice off the tops if they have domed, so they are all flat and the cake will stack more evenly (see also Top Tip).

9. For the frosting, whisk together all the ingredients, apart from the milk, until really smooth and creamy, adding the milk slowly, if needed, to reach a spreadable consistency.

10. To assemble the layer cake, place a smear of frosting on a serving plate and place one cake on top (this secures it in place). Spread over one-third of the frosting, then make a small indent in the middle. Fill this with some raspberry jam, then top with the second cake. Repeat with more frosting and jam, then place on the final cake. Spread over the rest of the frosting and swirl on the jam. Decorate with the raspberries and crushed pistachios.

11. Slice and enjoy the cake straight away. Cover leftovers tightly with cling film/plastic wrap or use a sealed container and refrigerate for 2–3 days. You can freeze the unfrosted cake sponges for 1 month (wrapped in cling film), then allow them to defrost before filling and decorating.

Dark Chocolate Brazil Nut Flapjacks

Makes 10 | **Prep time:** 10 minutes + 30 minutes cooling + 1–2 hours chilling | **Cook time:** 20 minutes

Everyone loves a good flapjack bar, and these ones tick all the nostalgic boxes of being "buttery-sweet", chewy, oaty and delicious while also being a great wholesome snack. These plant-based bars are packed with nutrition powerhouses like Brazil nuts, bananas, chia seeds and oats. The dark/bittersweet chocolate contains tryptophan which creates the happy hormone serotonin, so eating these bars may just boost your mood and mind!

For the flapjack mix

1 ripe banana (about 110g/3¾oz/½ cup)

90g/3¼oz/⅜ cup runny smooth almond butter

3 tbsp maple syrup

150g/5½oz/1½ cups rolled oats

12g/¼oz/½ cup puffed rice cereal

70g/2½oz/½ cup chopped Brazil nuts

4 Medjool dates, pitted and chopped (approx. 80g/2¾oz/½ cup once pitted)

2 tbsp hulled hemp seeds

2 tbsp chia seeds or ground flaxseed

½ tsp ground cinnamon

a pinch of salt

For the homemade chocolate top*

60g/2¼oz/½ cup cacao butter buttons (or coconut oil)

2 tbsp raw cacao powder

60g/2¼oz/¼ cup smooth cashew or almond butter

1 tbsp maple syrup

a pinch of salt

1. Preheat the oven to 190°C/375°F/Gas 5 and line a 15cm/6in square baking pan with baking parchment.

2. For the flapjack mix, mash the banana in a mixing bowl, then add the almond butter and maple syrup; stir until combined. Add the rest of the flapjack ingredients and stir really well. Pour the flapjack mix into the lined baking pan and press down firmly to make a smooth top.

4. Bake in the oven for 20 minutes, until it's smelling oaty and is golden brown on top. Allow to cool in the baking pan on a wire/cooling rack for 30 minutes.

5. Meanwhile, make the chocolate top. If making your own chocolate, add the cacao butter buttons to a heatproof bowl and melt in the microwave on High in 15-second bursts or over a pan of simmering water (known as a bain-marie) until just melted. Remove from the heat and whisk in the cacao powder, 2 tbsp of the cashew or almond butter, the maple syrup and salt. Whisk until really smooth.

6. Alternatively, use ready-made dark/bittersweet chocolate* and melt in the microwave or over a pan of simmering water as above. Pour the chocolate (whether homemade or ready-made) over the flapjack and fill in any gaps. Spoon over the rest of the cashew or almond butter and use a cocktail stick/toothpick to make swirls.

7. Place in the refrigerator to set for 1–2 hours until firm.

8. Remove the flapjack from the baking pan and use a sharp knife (I like to run it under hot water to warm the knife and then wipe it dry) to slice into 10 bars.

9. Enjoy straight away, or refrigerate in a sealed container for 1 week, or freeze for 1 month, then defrost before eating.

Top Tip

*Or as an alternative flavour combination for the top, try 115g/4oz of your favourite dark/bittersweet chocolate, finely chopped and melted with 1 tbsp of coconut oil, with 2 tbsp of almond butter for the swirls.

Top Tip
You can use other
fruits for the jam
filling, like blueberries or
strawberries, following the
same method as above.
Alternatively, use shop-
bought cherry (or
other fruit) jam for
the filling.

Cherry Coconut Oat Crumble Slices

Makes 9–16 | **Prep time:** 15 minutes + cooling
Cook time: 35 minutes (15 minutes for jam; 20 minutes for slices)

These dessert slices are wholesome enough for breakfast but delicious enough to serve to friends and family after dinner. They are packed with mind-boosting ingredients like wholegrain oats to allow for the gradual release of sugar into the bloodstream, keeping energy levels stable, plus bananas that contain vitamin B6 which is important for keeping your immune system healthy and synthesizing the feel-hormones serotonin and dopamine.

For the cherry chia jam

400g/14oz/2¾ cups fresh cherries (any in season), pitted weight (approx. 2 punnets)

4 tbsp maple syrup

1 tsp vanilla extract

4 tbsp chia seeds

For the oat slices

1 ripe banana, mashed well

4 tbsp maple syrup

4 tbsp runny smooth almond butter

4 tbsp melted coconut oil

1 tsp vanilla extract

150g/5½oz/1½ cups oat flour

150g/5½oz/1½ cups rolled oats

4 tbsp desiccated coconut

2 tbsp hulled hemp seeds

1 tsp ground cinnamon

1 tsp baking powder

a pinch of salt

For the crumble topping

50g/1¾oz/½ cup rolled oats

2 tbsp desiccated coconut

1. Start by making the jam as it needs to cool slightly. Add the pitted cherries, maple syrup and vanilla to a saucepan and bring to the boil over a high heat. Cook with a lid on, stirring occasionally, for 10 minutes, then remove the lid and cook for 5 minutes more. The cherries will be sticky and glossy. Put the cherries and chia seeds in a blender and blend until smooth. Pour into a heatproof jar and cool for 30 minutes.

2. Preheat the oven to 180°C/350°F/Gas 4 and line a 20cm/8in square baking pan with baking parchment.

3. For the oat slices, stir together the mashed banana, maple syrup, almond butter, coconut oil and vanilla in a large mixing bowl until smooth. Now add all the remaining ingredients and stir to a sticky mix. Press three-quarters of the mix into the base of the lined baking pan and evenly smooth over the top. Bake in the oven for 5 minutes.

4. Meanwhile, add the oats and desiccated coconut for the crumble topping to the rest of the oat mix and stir well.

5. Remove the baking pan from the oven (leave the oven on) and spread the cherry chia jam all over the base. Sprinkle over the topping and press down lightly. Return to the oven for 15 minutes until the top is golden brown.

6. Remove from the oven and cool on a wire/cooling rack for 20 minutes, before carefully lifting out the mixture and cooling fully on the rack.

7. Use a large, sharp knife to slice into 9 or 16 squares and eat straight away. Refrigerate leftover bars in a sealed container for 3–5 days. You can also freeze the bars for 1 month, wrapped well, then defrost before eating.

Chocolate Chunk Tahini Cookies

Makes 12 │ **Prep time:** 15 minutes + 10 minutes cooling/resting │ **Cook time:** 10 minutes

Chocolate chip cookies are the ultimate nostalgic bake. I love baking these for friends; they just make me feel so happy, and I've no doubt they will give you joy, too. These quick and easy cookies have a chewy middle and a golden, crispy outside and are filled with chunks of melting mood-boosting dark/bittersweet chocolate. No one will ever be able to tell that they are egg-free, gluten-free and gut-healthy, too, thanks to the fibre-rich flaxseed and polyphenol-rich dark chocolate.

For the cookies

1 tbsp ground flaxseed

2½ tbsp water

4 tbsp runny smooth tahini

75g/2¾oz/½ cup coconut sugar

2 tbsp olive oil or melted coconut oil

1 tbsp plant-based milk

1 tsp vanilla extract

200g/7oz/2 cups oat flour

¼ tsp bicarbonate of soda/baking soda

a pinch of salt

80g/2¾oz/heaped ½ cup dark/bittersweet chocolate chunks, plus (optional) extra for the tops

1. Preheat the oven to 180°C/350°F/Gas 4 and line two baking sheets with baking parchment.

2. Stir together the ground flaxseed and water and leave to rest for 5 minutes to make a gloopy gel.

3. In a large mixing bowl, whisk together the flaxseed gel, the tahini, coconut sugar, olive or coconut oil, milk and vanilla until smooth. Now add the oat flour, bicarbonate of soda and salt and stir to a sticky cookie dough.

4. Fold in the chocolate chunks and then divide the mix into 12 balls.

5. Using your hands, roll the balls into circles and flatten each one down slightly onto the lined baking sheets (wash your hands in between as they will get sticky!), leaving a 2cm/¾in space between each one.

6. Bake in the oven for 10 minutes, turning the baking sheets around after 5 minutes to ensure the cookies bake evenly. They will smell fragrant and will be golden at the edges.

7. If desired, as soon as the cookies are out of the oven, add a few extra small chunks of dark chocolate on top.

8. Allow the cookies to rest for 10 minutes and then enjoy warm, or allow to cool fully on the baking sheets.

9. Store the cookies in a sealed container at room temperature for 3–5 days, or freeze for 1 month, then defrost before eating.

Baked Vegan Jam Doughnuts

Makes 5–6 | **Prep time:** 25 minutes + 25 minutes proofing + cooling | **Cook time:** 21 minutes

Doughnuts are one of life's little joys and these baked (not fried) egg-free and plant-based doughnuts are delicious. They are packed with gooey homemade chia berry jam and they have the best glaze. They are ready in a few simple steps and are fun to bake for friends and family. The chia seeds in the jam are great for adding omega-3 fatty acids, while the abundance of fresh berries add antioxidants, vitamins and minerals to these mood-boosting bakes.

For the raspberry chia seed jam

180g/6¼oz/1½ cups fresh raspberries

½ tbsp lemon juice

½ tbsp coconut sugar

1 tbsp chia seeds

For the doughnuts

240ml/8½fl oz/1 cup plant-based milk

2 tbsp coconut oil or vegan butter

3 tbsp olive oil, plus extra for greasing

1 tbsp coconut sugar

2¼ tsp (7g/1/8oz, or 1 sachet) fast-action dried yeast

175g/6oz/1¼ cups plain/all-purpose flour, plus extra for dusting

175g/6oz/1¼ cups strong white bread flour

1 tsp salt

For the glaze and decoration

80g/2¾oz/½ cup icing/confectioners' sugar

6–12 fresh raspberries

1. Prepare the raspberry chia seed jam first so it can cool down. Add the raspberries, lemon juice and coconut sugar to a small saucepan and cook over a high heat for about 5 minutes, stirring often to break down the berries, until juicy. Remove from the heat and stir through the chia seeds. Pour into a heatproof container and allow to cool for 30 minutes. This jam will keep in a sealed container in the refrigerator for 3–5 days.

2. Meanwhile, make the dough. Warm the milk and coconut oil or butter in the microwave on Medium in 15-second bursts (for about 1 minute) until just melted, or in a saucepan, stirring occasionally. Whisk in 2 tbsp of the olive oil and the coconut sugar and check that the mix is lukewarm (you may need to let it cool down). Now sprinkle over the yeast and leave to activate for 5 minutes (it will start to become frothy and turn paler).

3. In a large mixing bowl, combine both flours and the salt. Now pour in the milky yeast mix and stir to a shaggy dough. Tip out onto a lightly floured work surface and knead for 1–2 minutes until smooth. Lightly grease a large bowl with olive oil, place the dough inside, cover loosely with a dish towel or cling film/plastic wrap and leave somewhere warm to rise for 25 minutes.

4. Preheat the oven to 180°C/350°F/Gas 4 and line a large baking sheet with baking parchment.

Method continues overleaf

5. Lightly flour the work surface again and tip out the dough on top. Gently roll out to 3cm/1¼in thickness (don't roll too much) and flour an 8cm/3¼in round cookie cutter. Cut out the doughnuts (you'll make 5 or 6), re-rolling any scraps as needed. Gently transfer them to the lined baking sheet and brush with the remaining 1 tbsp of olive oil.

6. Bake in the oven for about 16 minutes, or until well-risen, golden brown and baked through. Turn the baking sheet around halfway through to ensure they bake evenly.

7. Remove from the oven and place the baking sheet on a wire/cooling rack, leave to rest for 10 minutes, then transfer the doughnuts to the wire rack and leave to cool fully.

8. Prepare the glaze by mixing the icing sugar with 1 tbsp of the raspberry jam in a small bowl until thick. Place the rest of the jam in a piping/pastry bag fitted with a small round nozzle/tip.

9. Once the doughnuts are cool, spread the glaze over the tops. Now insert a chopstick through to the middle of each doughnut and wiggle around to make a hole. Pipe some jam into each hole until it just overflows. Decorate the doughnuts with the fresh raspberries.

10. Enjoy straight away, or later the same day. Refrigerate the doughnuts in a sealed container for 1 day, but enjoy them at room temperature.

Top Tips

You can use a small cutter (e.g. 5cm/2in) to make smaller doughnut bites and bake them in the oven for 12–14 minutes. You can also make any berry jam you like by swapping the raspberries for blueberries or strawberries. Please note, this recipe will not work with gluten-free flour.

Sun-dried Tomato Pesto and Spinach Babka

Serves 8 | **Prep time:** 25 minutes + 30 minutes proofing + cooling | **Cook time:** 35 minutes

This babka bread is a taste of the Mediterranean with a delicious sun-dried tomato pesto and wilted spinach filling. It is loaded with gut-healthy ingredients like olive oil, sunflower seeds and sun-dried tomatoes, which are also high in monounsaturated fats. These increase the diversity of our microbiome, positively impacting our mood. As well as being a mood-booster, this babka bread is fun to make and share with friends and family, is ready in an hour, plus it's naturally plant-based, egg-free and dairy-free.

For the dough

240ml/8½fl oz/1 cup plant-based milk

2 tbsp coconut oil

2 tbsp + 1 tsp olive oil, plus extra for greasing

1 tbsp coconut sugar

2¼ tsp (7g/1/8oz, or 1 sachet) fast-action dried yeast

175g/6oz/1¼ cups plain/ all-purpose flour, plus extra for dusting

175g/6oz/1¼ cups strong white bread flour

1 tsp salt

For the sun-dried tomato pesto

80g/2¾oz/½ cup sunflower seeds

1 garlic clove, peeled

2 tbsp nutritional yeast

80g/2¾oz/½ cup sun-dried tomatoes from a jar (drained weight)

2 tbsp tomato purée/paste

20g/¾oz/½ cup fresh basil, leaves and small stalks

2 tbsp lemon juice

2 tbsp olive oil

salt and pepper, to taste

For the filling

120g/4¼oz/2 cups baby spinach

1. Start by making the dough. Warm the milk and coconut oil in the microwave on Medium in 15-second bursts (for about 1 minute) until just melted, or in a saucepan, stirring occasionally. Whisk in the 2 tbsp of olive oil and the coconut sugar and check that the mix is lukewarm (let it cool down if needed). Now sprinkle over the yeast and leave to activate for 5 minutes (it will start to become frothy and turn paler).

2. In a large mixing bowl, combine both flours and the salt. Now pour in the milky yeast mix and stir to a shaggy dough. Tip onto a lightly floured work surface and knead for 1–2 minutes until smooth. Lightly grease a large bowl with olive oil, place the dough inside, cover loosely with a dish towel or cling film/plastic wrap and leave somewhere warm to rise for 30 minutes (see Top Tips).

3. Meanwhile, make the pesto. Add all the ingredients to a small blender or food processor and blitz to a smooth but slightly chunky pesto. Season to taste with salt and pepper. Spoon the pesto into a container, cover and refrigerate for 3–5 days (if making in advance).

4. To prepare the spinach, heat a large, dry non-stick frying pan over a high heat and add all the spinach. Stir well and allow to wilt until it's dark green and reduced a lot, about 2–3 minutes. Transfer the spinach to a sieve/fine mesh strainer and squeeze out all the excess water – you will be left with 40g/1½oz/¼ cup of spinach. Roughly chop this up.

5. Preheat the oven to 180°C/350°F/Gas 4. Grease and line a loaf pan (approx. 10 x 20cm/4 x 8in) with baking parchment.

6. Once the dough has risen, lightly flour the work surface again and tip out the dough. Roll out to a rectangle (approx. 36 x 30cm/14¼ x 12in) and spread over 240g/8½oz/1 cup of the pesto. Sprinkle over the spinach.

7. From a longer side, roll up the dough fairly tightly to form a long roll. Slice the roll in half lengthways into two strips, leaving the very top 2cm/¾in intact. Carefully plait/braid the two strands of dough together until you reach the end.

8. Squish both ends inward as you lift up the babka dough and nestle it into the lined loaf pan (tuck the ends underneath, if needed).

9. Brush all over the top with the remaining 1 tsp of olive oil, then bake in the oven for 35 minutes until well-risen and golden brown.

10. Remove from the oven and allow the babka to cool in the loaf pan for 10 minutes, then lift it out and cool fully on a wire/cooling rack.

11. Enjoy warm or allow to cool, and slice the babka bread into chunks. It's also great brushed with extra olive oil on top to serve.

12. This is best enjoyed on the same day, but refrigerate any leftover babka in a sealed container for 1–2 days, or wrap well in cling film/plastic wrap and freeze for 1 month, then defrost before eating.

Top Tips

This babka bread is much quicker to make than most yeasted dough recipes, so keep in mind that the quick rise/proof will not cause the bread to double, only increase in size slightly. Please note, this recipe will not work with gluten-free flour.

No Nuts Homemade Cream Cheese

Serves 4 | **Prep time:** 10 minutes + 30 minutes chilling + cooling

It doesn't get better than homemade cream cheese and this recipe has two flavour options: garlic and herb or sweet chilli – they are both delicious! It comes together in less than 10 minutes and contains no nuts, making both flavour options ideal for everyone to share – spread the cream cheese on crackers, toast or bread, or serve as a dip with vegetable sticks. This recipe is loaded with gut-healthy ingredients like tofu, coconut yogurt and miso paste, which are fermented foods to help feed the gut and increase our microbiome diversity.

For the homemade cream cheese

1 x 200g/7oz block of extra-firm tofu, drained

2 tbsp coconut oil, melted and cooled

2 tbsp thick coconut yogurt

1 tbsp lemon juice

½ tbsp white miso paste

½ tbsp nutritional yeast

½ tsp salt

1–2 tbsp plant-based milk

For the garlic and herb flavour

1 garlic clove, crushed

1 spring onion/scallion, finely sliced

1 tbsp chopped fresh chives

black pepper, to taste

a drizzle of olive oil, to serve

For the sweet chilli flavour

½–1 tsp chilli flakes

2 tsp maple syrup, plus extra to serve

1. For the homemade cream cheese, break up the tofu into a food processor and add the coconut oil, coconut yogurt, lemon juice, miso paste, nutritional yeast and salt. Blend together until starting to become smooth, then slowly add the milk to reach a smooth consistency (it will be slightly thicker than shop-bought cream cheese). Stop to scrape down the sides as necessary.

2. Pour the mixture into a bowl and stir in all the ingredients for either the garlic and herb flavour, or for the sweet chilli flavour.

3. Cover tightly and refrigerate for 30 minutes to allow the flavours to infuse (it will also thicken slightly more).

4. Serve the garlic and herb flavour with a drizzle of olive oil, and the sweet chilli one with some extra maple syrup on top, and enjoy. This is great spread on crackers, bread and toast, enjoyed as part of a mezze board or stirred into hot pasta or other cooked whole grains.

5. Keep refrigerated in a sealed container for 3–5 days.

Top Tip

You can make both flavours at the same time simply by doubling the homemade cream cheese base recipe, then dividing the mixture into two bowls and adding the mix-ins as above.

Top Tips

You can add other nuts (like pecans or walnuts) or seeds (like sunflower or pumpkin seeds) into these brownies instead of the hazelnuts. And try playing around with the flavour by using flavoured dark/ bittersweet chocolate (such as raspberry or salted caramel).

Fudgy Chickpea Hazelnut Chocolate Brownies

Makes 9–16 | **Prep time:** 20 minutes + cooling | **Cook time:** 30 minutes

Nothing beats a warm gooey chocolate fudge brownie and these ones are complete with a luscious two-ingredient chocolate ganache that will have you dreaming of healthier bakes. No one will be able to tell that these brownies are made from high-fibre, high-protein chickpeas/garbanzo beans, nor that they are flourless and grain-free. The peanut butter, hazelnuts and coconut yogurt are natural mood-boosters, while the cocoa and dark/bittersweet chocolate act as mood stimulants, as they contain high levels of polyphenols, which feed the gut microbiome.

For the brownies

1 x 400g/14oz can chickpeas/garbanzo beans, drained, rinsed and patted dry (240g/8½oz/1½ cups drained weight)

120g/4¼oz/½ cup runny smooth peanut butter

1 ripe banana

4 tbsp maple syrup

2 tbsp olive oil

50g/1¾oz/½ cup unsweetened cocoa powder

¼ tsp bicarbonate of soda/baking soda

a pinch of salt

85g/3oz dark/bittersweet chocolate chips

70g/2½oz/½ cup raw blanched hazelnuts, chopped

For the chocolate ganache

125g/4½oz dark/bittersweet chocolate chips

2 tbsp thick coconut yogurt or coconut cream

To finish

2 tbsp raw blanched hazelnuts, roughly chopped

flaky salt, to taste

1. Preheat the oven to 180°C/350°F/Gas 4 and line a 20cm/8in square baking pan with baking parchment.

2. For the brownies, add the chickpeas to a high-speed food processor or blender along with the peanut butter, banana, maple syrup, olive oil, cocoa powder, bicarbonate of soda and salt. Blend until really smooth and no lumps of chickpea remain. Stop to scrape down the sides as necessary. Pour in the chocolate chips and hazelnuts and stir through.

3. Spoon the thick batter into the lined baking pan and smooth over the top. Bake in the oven for 30 minutes. When it's ready, an inserted skewer will come out clean around the edges of the bake, but the middle will still be fudgy.

4. Allow the baked brownie to cool in the baking pan for 20 minutes, then lift out and leave to cool for a further 1 hour on a wire/cooling rack.

5. When the baked brownie is cool enough to handle, prepare the ganache. Melt the chocolate chips in a heatproof bowl in the microwave on High in 15-second bursts or over a pan of simmering water (known as a bain-marie), and once smooth, stir in the coconut yogurt or cream until smooth and glossy.

6. Spread the ganache over the baked brownie, then sprinkle over the hazelnuts and some flaky salt. Slice into 9 or 16 squares and enjoy the brownies slightly warm or allow to cool completely before eating.

7. Once cool, refrigerate the brownies in a sealed container for 2–3 days. You can also freeze the brownies for 1 month, wrapped well, then defrost before eating.

Blackberry and Lemon Cupcakes

Makes 12 | **Prep time:** 15 minutes + cooling | **Cook time:** 20–22 minutes

These cupcakes are fluffy, golden and bursting with antioxidant-rich blackberries and zesty lemon. They contain mood-boosting foods like oats which slowly release energy to maintain blood sugar, coconut yogurt to feed your gut microbes, and tahini which contains amino acids to support production of serotonin. These are perfect little bakes for celebrations. I've included two choices of frosting: I like to make a buttercream frosting, but for an everyday bake I love the yogurt option as a light, gut-friendly cupcake topper.

Top Tip
*To make these cupcakes gluten-free, ensure your flour blend contains xanthan gum, but if it doesn't, add ½ tsp of xanthan gum to the 210g/7 ½oz/1 ½ cups of gluten-free flour for the cupcakes, and use gluten-free baking powder.

For the cupcakes

2 tbsp ground flaxseed or chia seeds

300g/10½oz/2 heaped cups fresh blackberries, plus 24 extra to garnish

210g/7½oz/1½ cups + 1 tsp plain/all-purpose flour or gluten-free* plain/all-purpose flour

200g/7oz/generous ¾ cup unsweetened apple sauce or mashed banana

160g/5¾oz/2/3 cup thick coconut yogurt

60g/2¼oz/¼ cup runny smooth tahini

60ml/2fl oz/¼ cup olive oil

110g/3¾oz/¾ cup coconut sugar

1 tsp apple cider vinegar

1 tsp vanilla extract

grated zest of 1 lemon

100g/3½oz/1 cup oat flour

1 tsp baking powder

½ tsp bicarbonate of soda/baking soda

a pinch of salt

For the buttercream frosting

120g/4¼oz/½ cup vegan butter

300g/10½oz/3 cups icing/confectioners' sugar

1–2 tbsp plant-based milk

½ tsp vanilla extract

grated zest of 1 lemon

OR For the yogurt frosting

240g/8½oz/1 cup thick coconut yogurt

30g/1oz/¼ cup vegan vanilla protein powder

1 tbsp maple syrup

1–2 tbsp plant-based milk

grated zest of 1 lemon

1. Preheat the oven to 180°C/350°F/Gas 4 and line a muffin pan with 12 paper muffin cases/liners.

2. For the cupcakes, stir together the ground flaxseed or chia seeds with 5 tbsp water and leave for 5 minutes to form a gel.

3. Toss the blackberries in the 1 tsp of plain flour and leave to one side.

4. In a large mixing bowl, whisk together the flax/chia gel, the apple sauce or banana, coconut yogurt, tahini, olive oil, coconut sugar, vinegar, vanilla and lemon zest until smooth. Sift in the remaining plain flour, then add the oat flour, baking powder, bicarbonate of soda and salt. Whisk again to a thick, smooth batter.

5. Fold the blackberries into the batter, being careful not to over-mix.

6. Use a large spoon or ice-cream scoop to divide the batter evenly between the paper cases, filling each almost to the top. Smooth over the tops with a spoon.

7. Bake in the oven for 20–22 minutes until well-risen, golden on top and an inserted skewer comes out clean.

8. Carefully remove the cupcakes from the muffin pan and allow to cool fully on a wire/cooling rack.

9. For the buttercream frosting, allow the butter to rest at room temperature for an hour, to soften, and then add to the large bowl of a stand mixer (or use an electric hand-held mixer) and beat until smooth. Gradually add in the icing sugar, milk, vanilla and lemon zest, while beating, to create a smooth and creamy frosting. Continue to beat for 1–2 minutes to make it really soft.

10. Or, if you are making the yogurt frosting, add all the ingredients to a large bowl and whisk together until smooth.

11. To decorate, put the frosting into a piping/pastry bag with a star-shaped (or other) nozzle/tip and pipe it on top of the cooled cupcakes. Decorate with the fresh blackberries and add crushed pistachios, if you like.

12. Enjoy straight away, or refrigerate in a sealed container for 3–5 days. You can also freeze the cupcakes, without the frosting, for 1 month, then defrost before decorating.

Chocolate Banoffee Caramel Slices

Makes 9 | **Prep time:** 20 minutes + 1–1½ hours chilling

Caramel slices are a throwback to my childhood and my love for all things banoffee and chocolate. These no-bake, gluten-free chocolate caramel slices are just as indulgent as your favourite childhood treats yet they're made with wholesome ingredients like fibre-rich oats and polyphenol-packed dark chocolate, as well as a fibre- and protein-rich base and filling. They melt in your mouth and make a perfect feel-good dessert or snack.

For the base

60g/2¼oz/¼ cup runny
  smooth peanut butter

2 tbsp maple syrup

2 tbsp melted coconut oil

150g/5½oz/1½ cups oat flour

50g/1¾oz/½ cup
  ground almonds

a pinch of salt

For the caramel middle

80g/2¾oz/⅓ cup runny
  smooth peanut butter

80ml/2¾fl oz/⅓ cup
  maple syrup

3 tbsp melted coconut oil

½ tsp ground cinnamon

a pinch of salt

1 banana, sliced
  into 16 rounds

For the chocolate top

100g/3½oz dark/bittersweet
  chocolate, finely chopped

1 tbsp coconut oil

2 tbsp runny smooth
  peanut butter

2 tbsp banana chips/
  coins (dried banana
  slices) (optional)

flaky salt, to finish

1. Line a 15cm/6in square baking pan with baking parchment.

2. First, make the base. In a medium mixing bowl, stir together the peanut butter, maple syrup and coconut oil until smooth. Now add the oat flour, ground almonds and salt and stir to a sticky mix. Put this cookie dough-like mix into the lined baking pan and press down firmly to make a compact base. Chill in the refrigerator while you move on.

3. Next, make the caramel for the middle. In a small bowl, stir together the peanut butter, maple syrup, coconut oil, cinnamon and salt until really smooth.

4. Remove the baking pan from the refrigerator and lay over the banana slices in a single layer. Pour over the caramel and smooth out so all the banana slices are covered. Return the pan to the refrigerator to set for 30–60 minutes.

5. For the chocolate top, melt together the chocolate and coconut oil in a heatproof bowl over a pan of simmering water (known as a bain-marie) or in the microwave on High in 15-second bursts, until glossy.

6. Remove the caramel bar mixture from the refrigerator and pour over the chocolate, ensuring to fill in all the corners. Now drop spoonfuls of the peanut butter over the top and use a cocktail stick/toothpick or spoon to make swirly patterns. Add on some banana chips/coins, if you like, then chill in the refrigerator for 30 more minutes, or until firm to touch. Sprinkle over a little flaky salt just before serving.

7. When ready to serve, lift the bar mixture out of the baking pan and use a warmed sharp knife to slice it into 9 squares.

8. Enjoy straight away, or refrigerate these slices in a sealed container for 1 week, or freeze for 1 month, then defrost before eating.

Top Tip
Make these slices
nut-free by using
sunflower seed butter
or runny smooth tahini
instead of the peanut
butter, and use extra oat
flour in place of the
ground almonds.

about the author

Amy Lanza is the full-time recipe developer, content creator and food photographer behind Nourishing Amy, who is passionate about plant-based and holistic wellbeing. She promotes a mindful and balanced approach to health, focusing on vibrant and delicious recipes, with the aim of making it easy, accessible and enjoyable to eat a more plant-based diet. Her work has been featured in numerous magazines like *Vegan Life, Thrive Mags, Waitrose Weekend* and more. She is the author of *Nourishing Vegan Every Day* as well as two self-published eBooks and has an engaged loyal following across her social media accounts and website.

acknowledgments

This book would not have been possible without my amazing family and friends who have supported me, not only while creating this cookbook, but also on my journey to becoming a full-time content creator. To mum and dad for your endless testing of each and every recipe, and for your unwavering belief in my dreams and in me, this book would not be here without you. Thank you for being my number one fans, for listening to my endless list of recipe ideas and for reminding me of how far I have come. I am also rather grateful for you allowing me to make so much mess in the kitchen, and for helping out with the washing up.

To my wider family, friends and neighbours, who have always encouraged me, thank you for (often unknowingly) tasting these recipes and providing honest feedback. I appreciate your commitment to Feel Good Kitchen, to spread the message of plant-based goodness and for trying something new. For those who aren't vegan, you have given me a new perspective and input into how this book can be most useful and appealing to readers.

A big thank you to Eli Brecher, Registered Associate Nutritionist (ANutr) specialising in gut health, who I have had the pleasure of meeting multiple times. Eli has worked so hard to make sure all of the nutritional elements of the book are accurate, so you have the tools to make the most informed decisions on what to eat, and how each recipe will benefit you.

This book would never be in your hands without the incredible team at Watkins Publishers. A few years ago, Watkins approached with me an idea, and I asked them to wait a year or so while I worked on book one, and so here we are. Over that time, the scope and feel of the book has developed and grown into something I'd only ever dreamed of. The two parts of Happy Mind and Healthy Brain work seamlessly together and sharing the nutritional information alongside delicious recipes is something I am so proud of. Thank you for your passion and enthusiasm for this project in creating this book. Another thanks to the amazing design team and copy editors who have allowed the photography and recipes to shine.

Finally, a massive thank you to YOU for holding this book in your hands. As a content creator, food photographer and recipe developer, without you watching my videos, following me on social media and re-creating my recipes, I really would not be where I am today. You have made this second cookbook a reality and I hope you will enjoy this cookbook as much as I have loved creating it for us all.

INDEX

A

agave syrup 17
ageing 10, 34
almond 12, 41, 48, 62, 159
almond butter 92, 109, 120, 124, 186, 189
almond (ground) 129, 204
amino acids 12
anthocyanins 13
anti-inflammatories 12, 79
antioxidants 10, 30, 38, 41, 44, 50, 52, 62, 66, 70, 72, 74, 76, 79–80, 82, 86, 92, 95, 102, 108, 120, 140, 144, 152, 154, 162, 164, 166, 168, 172, 174, 193, 202
anxiety 12
apple, date and nut breakfast oat cups 124, **125**
apple cider vinegar 15
apple sauce 16, 107, 124, 130, 203
asparagus, lemony asparagus salad with avocado cream **64**, 65
aubergine
    roasted aubergine and broccoli lentil curry 74–5, **74**
    sticky miso mushrooms and aubergines with creamy butter beans 176–7, **176**
avocado 10, 13, 38–9, 56, 82, 107, 148, 151, 159
    avocado cream **64**, 65
    avocado, strawberry and chickpea salad 48, **49**
    dark chocolate avocado pistachio truffles 96, **97**
    guacamole 59, 171
    high-protein avocado toast with crispy chickpeas 30–1, **30**
    red lentil pancakes with black beans and avocado 34–5, **34**
    tomatoes and avocado salsa **42**, 43

B

babka, sun-dried tomato pesto and spinach 195–7, **195**, **197**
bagels, cinnamon raisin and garlic chive (no-yeast!) 126–7, **126**
banana 12, 14, 36, 107, 110, 133, 136, 186, 189, 201, 203
    banana nut cinnamon rolls 122–3, **122**
    caramelised banana 36, **37**
    chocolate banana oat flour crêpes 134, **135**
    chocolate banoffee caramel slices 204, **205**
    chocolate chip peanut butter banana bread 128–9, **128**
    matcha pistachio creamy oats 28, **29**
    mint chocolate chip smoothie 121
    mocha date shake 120
    peanut butter and berry smoothie 121
basil 50, 53, 81, 89, 163
bean(s) 15
    beany Mediterranean orzo salad 156, **157**
    black bean mango salsa taco bowls 178–9, **178**
    butter bean and tofu feta shakshuka 32, **33**
    creamy arrabbiata beans **88**, 89
    hidden vegetable squash and tomato soup 144
    Mediterranean nourish bowls 87
    mushroom, bean and lentil chilli 170–1, **170**
    red lentil pancakes with black beans and avocado 34–5, **34**
    roasted vegetable and salsa verde bean sandwich 52–3, **52**
    spinach and tofu curry with coconut rice 175
    sticky miso mushrooms and aubergines with creamy butter beans 176–7, **176**
    white bean and kale soup 50, **51**
    see also edamame
beetroot hummus with lentils and pistachios 152, **153**
berries 10, 14
    peanut butter and berry smoothie **118–19**, 121, **121**
    see also specific berries
beta carotene 72
Black Forest lava cakes 102–3, **102**
blackberry and lemon cupcakes 202–3, **202**
blood flow, healthy 10, 38, 58, 96
blood pressure reduction 10, 30, 43, 65, 92
blood sugar regulation 12, 202
brain cells 10, 52, 102
Brain Health 9, 10, 20, 23–110
    breakfast & brunch for 24–44
    desserts for 90–110
    dinner for 68–89
    lunch for 46–66
    snacks for 90–110
brain plasticity 10, 102
Brazil nut 12, 143
bread (ready-made) 39

croutons 50, **51**
French toast **132**, 133
roasted vegetable and
salsa verde bean
sandwich 52–3, **52**
breakfast & brunch 24–44,
114–36
broccoli 10, 140, 143, 159, 167
roasted aubergine and
broccoli lentil curry 74–5,
74
broccoli (long-stemmed) 151,
167
brownies
edible brownie cookie
dough jars 100, **101**
fudgy chickpea hazelnut
chocolate brownies **200**,
201
brunch *see* breakfast &
brunch
Brussels sprouts 55
sprout salad 62, **63**
buckwheat 16
buckwheat flour 17, 104, 134,
155, 163, 169, 173
superfood buckwheat and
seed bread **94**, 95
buckwheat groats 41, 44
bulgur wheat 16
butter (vegan) 15
buttercream frosting **202**, 203
butternut squash 167
creamy roasted butternut
squash and spinach dahl
76–7, **76**
hidden vegetable squash
and tomato soup 144, **145**
roasted squash and tofu
sprout salad 62, **63**

c

cabbage *see* red cabbage
cacao butter buttons
dark chocolate Brazil nut
flapjacks 186
homemade dark chocolate
bars three ways 92, **93**
cacao nibs 44, 120, 121
cacao powder 15–16, 100, 116

cacao pistachio brain
booster creamy oats **40**,
41
chocolate breakfast
mousse 36
dark chocolate avocado
pistachio truffles 96
dark chocolate Brazil nut
flapjacks 186
homemade dark chocolate
bars three ways 92
Caesar dressing 150–1, **150**
caffeine 10, 102, 120
cakes
Black Forest lava cakes
102–3, **102**
blackberry and lemon
cupcakes 202–3, **202**
chocolate chip peanut
butter banana bread
128–9, **128**
espresso walnut cake bars
110, **111**
hidden vegetable chocolate
fudge cake 106–7, **106**
raspberry ripple layer cake
184–5, **185**
calcium 10, 80
caramel
caramelised banana and
nuts 36, **37**
caramelized peach and
vanilla pancakes 136, **137**
chocolate banoffee
caramel slices 204, **205**
carotenoids 10
carrot 50, 85, 140, 144, 146,
148, 167
roasted carrot and
chickpea kale bowls 82,
83
cashew nut 12, 109
cashew nut butter 92, 186
cauliflower
cauliflower gnocchi with
red pepper sauce 162–3,
162
Moroccan-inspired roasted
cauliflower salad 54–5,
54

roasted cauliflower nuggets
with tzatziki 168–9, **168**
cavolo nero 48, 50, 56, 62, 66,
72, 79, 82, 143, 151
cheesecake, strawberry
cheesecake French toast
132–3, **132**
cherry
Black Forest lava cakes 103
cherry Bakewell brain
booster creamy oats **40**,
41
cherry chia jam **188**, 189
cherry coconut oat
crumbles slices **188**, 189
chia seed 10
apple, date and nut
breakfast oat cups 124
blackberry and lemon
cupcakes 203
brain booster creamy oats
three ways 41
brain food granola 27
caramelized peach and
vanilla pancakes 136
cherry chia jam **188**, 189
dark chocolate Brazil nut
flapjacks 186
espresso walnut cake bars
110
French toast 133
grain-free high-protein
Bircher muesli 44
lentil and mushroom
`meatballs' with
homemade tomato sauce
181
matcha pistachio creamy
oats 28
Neapolitan chia pudding
116, **117**
raspberry chia seed jam
192, 193–4
raspberry jam 184–5
raspberry ripple layer cake
184–5
superfood buckwheat and
seed bread 95
chickpea/garbanzo bean
avocado, strawberry and

chickpea salad 48, **49**
beany Mediterranean orzo
    salad 156
beetroot hummus with
    lentils and pistachios 152
edible brownie cookie
    dough jars 100
fudgy chickpea hazelnut
    chocolate brownies **200**,
    201
herby hummus **142**, 143
high-protein avocado toast
    with crispy chickpeas
    30–1, **30**
homemade hummus 159
Moroccan-inspired roasted
    cauliflower salad 54–5
nutty orange brain-food
    slaw 56
red pepper pesto chickpea
    traybake **78**, 79
roasted carrot and
    chickpea kale bowls 82,
    83
smoky red pepper pasta
    salad 66
spiced chickpea-stuffed
    sweet potatoes 72, **73**
sweet potato falafel wraps
    with herby tahini 155
sweet potato pizza 173
chickpea/gram flour 17, 35, 43,
    55, 60–1, 173
chilli (dish), mushroom, bean
    and lentil 170–1, **170**
chillies 14
    hot chilli sauce 15
chive 169
    garlic chive bagels (no-
    yeast!) 126–7, **126**
chocolate (dark/bittersweet)
    10, 13
    Black Forest lava cakes **102**,
    103
    cacao pistachio brain
    booster creamy oats 41
    chocolate banana oat flour
    crêpes 134, **135**
    chocolate banoffee
    caramel slices 204, **205**

chocolate breakfast
    mousse 36, **37**
chocolate chip peanut
    butter banana bread
    128–9, **128**
chocolate chunk tahini
    cookies 190, **191**
chocolate ganache **200**, 201
dark chocolate avocado
    pistachio truffles 96, **97**
dark chocolate Brazil nut
    flapjacks 186, **187**
edible brownie cookie
    dough jars 100
fudgy chickpea hazelnut
    chocolate brownies **200**,
    201
hidden vegetable chocolate
    fudge cake 106–7, **106**
homemade dark chocolate
    bars three ways 92, **93**
mint chocolate chip
    smoothie **119**, 121, **121**
mushroom, bean and lentil
    chilli 171
Neapolitan chia pudding
    116
Snickers-style protein bars
    98–9, **98**
tiramisu chocolate ganache
    tart 108–9, **108**
choline 54
cinnamon 27, 44, 110, 124, 130,
    133, 134, 136, 186, 189, 204
    banana nut cinnamon rolls
    122–3, **122**
    cinnamon raisin bagels
    (no-yeast!) 126–7, **126**
cocoa powder 15–16, 96, 100,
    103, 107, 109, 201
coconut 17
    cherry coconut oat
    crumbles slices **188**, 189
coconut cream 96, 109
coconut flour 17
coconut milk 15, 74–5, 77, 85,
    109, 144, 148, 167
    coconut rice 174–5, **174**
coconut sugar 17
coconut yogurt 12, 15

apple, date and nut
    breakfast oat cups 124
avocado cream 65
bagels 127
Black Forest lava cakes 103
blackberry and lemon
    cupcakes 203
brain booster creamy oats
    three ways 41
Caesar dressing 151
chocolate banana oat flour
    crêpes 134
chocolate breakfast
    mousse 36
chocolate chip peanut
    butter banana bread 129
chocolate ganache 201
creamy arrabbiata beans
    89
cucumber raita 70–1, 175
dark chocolate avocado
    pistachio truffles 96
espresso coffee frosting 110
espresso walnut cake bars
    110
frosting 107, 123, 185
grain-free high-protein
    Bircher muesli 44
herby tahini 155
herby yogurt 60–1, **60**
lime yogurt **34**, 35
matcha pistachio creamy
    oats 28
mint chocolate chip
    smoothie 121
mocha date shake 120
Neapolitan chia pudding
    116
no nuts homemade cream
    cheese 198
peanut butter and berry
    smoothie 121
raspberry ripple layer cake
    184–5
strawberry cheesecake
    yogurt **132**, 133
superfood buckwheat and
    seed bread 95
tahini yogurt **42**, 43
tzatziki 169

whipped tahini 59
yogurt frosting **202**, 203
coffee 10, 13, 103
  espresso walnut cake bars
      110, **111**
  mocha date shake 120
  tiramisu chocolate ganache
      tart 109
cognitive decline, prevention
    10, 30, 34, 38, 43, 65
cookies
  chocolate chunk tahini
      cookies 190, **191**
  cookie crumb **132**, 133
  edible brownie cookie
      dough jars 100, **101**
coriander/cilantro 39, 43,
    52–3, 55, 56, 59, 71, 72, 85,
    155, 175
courgette/zucchini 50, 53, 79,
    107, 120
  one-pan courgette lasagne
      164, **165**
  roasted courgette 81
couscous 16, 79
cream cheese (vegan) 15, 123
  frosting 123, 185
  no nuts homemade cream
      cheese 198, **199**
cream (dairy-free) 15
  avocado cream **64**, 65
crêpes, chocolate banana oat
    flour 134, **135**
croutons 50, **51**
crumble slices, cherry coconut
    oat **188**, 189
cucumber 65, 85, 146, 159, 169,
    175
  cucumber raita 70–1, **70**,
      174, 175
cupcakes, blackberry and
    lemon 202–3, **202**
curry
  golden miso curry noodle
      bowls 166–7, **166**
  miso curry sauce 167
  roasted aubergine and
      broccoli lentil curry 74–5,
      74
  spinach and tofu curry with

coconut rice 174–5, **174**
custard (dairy-free) 15

D
dahl, creamy roasted
    butternut squash and
    spinach 76–7, **76**
dairy-free essentials 15
date(s) 36, 55, 99, 121, 186
  apple, date and nut
      breakfast oat cups 124,
      125
  mocha date shake **118**, 120,
      120
depression 12, 13
desserts 90–110, 182–204
digestion 12, 140
dinner 68–89, 160–81
dopamine 12, 122, 128, 189
doughnuts, baked vegan jam
    192, 193–4
dressings 48, 55–6, 62, 156,
    179
  Caesar **150**, 151
  tahini 87
dukkah 54–5, **54**

E
`eating the rainbow' 12–13, 14
edamame
  kimchi edamame satay
      bowls 148, **149**
  veggie edamame fried rice
      with sticky tofu 140, **141**
espresso walnut cake bars
    110, **111**

F
falafel, sweet potato falafel
    wraps with herby tahini
    154–5, **154**
fats, healthy 10, 34, 44, 72, 98,
    154
  monounsaturated 10, 38,
      43, 52, 58, 60, 96, 152, 195
  see also omega-3 fatty
      acids
fermented foods 12, 16, 128,
    148, 158, 168, 198
`feta', butter bean and tofu

feta shakshuka 32, **33**
fibre 10, 12, 30, 34, 41, 43–4, 50,
    52, 58, 65, 72, 74, 82, 98, 100,
    104, 120, 124, 140, 144, 152,
    154, 156, 162, 168, 170, 172,
    176, 180, 201
flapjacks, dark chocolate
    Brazil nut 186, **187**
flavonoids 10, 13, 92, 98, 100,
    102, 108, 170, 184
flaxseed 10, 27, 44, 61, 95, 107,
    110, 129, 134, 173, 181, 186, 190,
    203
flours 17
  see also specific flours
folate 10
free radicals 10, 102
freekeh 16
freezer items 14
French toast, strawberry
    cheesecake 132–3, **132**
fresh produce 14
fritters, spinach lentil fritters
    with herby yogurt 60–1, **60**
frosting **106**, 107, 110, **111**, **122**,
    123, 185, **185**
  buttercream **202**, 203
  peanut butter 129
  yogurt **202**, 203
fruit 14
  see also specific fruit
fudgy chickpea hazelnut
    chocolate brownies **200**, 201

G
ganache
  chocolate ganache **200**, 201
  tiramisu chocolate ganache
      tart 108–9, **108**
garbanzo bean see chickpea/
    garbanzo bean
garlic
  garlic chive bagels (no-
      yeast!) 126–7, **126**
  no nuts homemade cream
      cheese 198
ginger 130
  ginger and rhubarb brain
      booster creamy oats **40**,
      41

glazes 130, **131**, **192**, 193–4
gnocchi, cauliflower gnocchi
     with red pepper sauce
     162–3, **162**
gochujang sauce **168**, 169
grains 16
     see also specific grains
granola, brain food **26**, 27
guacamole 58–9, **58**, **170**, 171
gut bacteria 60, 76, 116, 150,
     158, 168
gut health 12, 13
gut microbiome 12, 30, 43, 70,
     116, 134, 142, 156, 176, 178,
     195, 198, 201, 202
gut-brain axis 12, 44, 70, 76,
     124, 128, 140, 148, 150, 152,
     164, 184

H
`halloumi', sticky tofu halloumi
     glow bowls 158–9
`hanger' 12, 124
hazelnut 55, 134
     caramelised banana and
          nuts 36, **37**
     fudgy chickpea hazelnut
          chocolate brownies **200**,
          201
heart health 12
hemp seed 27–8, 30, 34–5, 41,
     44, 53, 66, 81, 95, 120–1, 146,
     173, 186
herbs 14
     dried 18
     herby hummus 142–3, **142**
     herby tahini 154–5, **154**, 155
     herby yogurt 60–1, **60**
     see also specific herbs
hobs/stovetops 19
hummus (homemade) 53, 146,
     155
     beetroot hummus with
          lentils and pistachios 152,
          153
     leaves, scrambled tofu
          hummus breakfast bowls
          39
     nutty pea quinoa hummus
          bowls 142–3, **142**
     recipe **158**, 159

I
ice cream (dairy-free) 15
immune system 72, 156, 189
iron 10, 80, 104

J
jam
     cherry chia **188**, 189
     raspberry 184–5, **185**
     raspberry chia seed **192**,
          193–4

K
kala namak (black sea salt) 18
kale 10, 48, 55–6, 72, 79, 143,
     163
     kale Caesar salad with
          crispy tofu 150–1, **150**
     roasted carrot and
          chickpea kale bowls 82,
          83
     white bean and kale soup
          50, **51**
kimchi 12, 16
     kimchi edamame satay
          bowls 148, **149**
kitchen gadgets 19

L
lasagne, one-pan courgette
     164, **165**
learning 10, 98, 102, 108
lemon 15
     blackberry and lemon
          cupcakes 202–3, **202**
     lemon yogurt frosting **202**,
          203
     lemony asparagus salad
          with avocado cream **64**,
          65
lentil(s)
     beetroot hummus with
          lentils and pistachios 152,
          153
     creamy roasted butternut
          squash and spinach dahl
          77
     lentil and mushroom
          `meatballs' with
          homemade tomato sauce
          180–1, **180**
     mushroom, bean and lentil
          chilli 170–1, **170**
     one-pan courgette lasagne
          164
     red lentil pancakes with
          black beans and avocado
          34–5, **34**
     roasted aubergine and
          broccoli lentil curry 74–5,
          74
     spinach lentil fritters with
          herby yogurt 60–1, **60**
lime 15, 59, 61, 71, 74–5, 77
     lime yogurt **34**, 35
lunch 46–66, 138–59

M
magnesium 13, 54, 150
mango, black bean mango
     salsa taco bowls 178–9, **178**
maple syrup 17
     hot maple **158**, 159
marinades 140, **141**
matcha pistachio creamy oats
     28, **29**
`meatballs', lentil and
     mushroom `meatballs' with
     homemade tomato sauce
     180–1, **180**
Mediterranean nourish bowls
     86–7, **86**
memory 10, 38, 58, 60, 62, 66,
     76, 96, 98, 102, 104, 108
menu planners 20
milks (dairy-free, plant-
     based) 15
Mind, Happy 9, 12–13, 20,
     113–204
     breakfast & brunch for
          114–36
     desserts for 182–204
     dinner for 160–81
     lunch for 138–59
     snacks for 182–204
mint 48, 53, 55–6, 71, 85, 155,
     169
     mint chocolate chip
          smoothie **119**, 121, **121**
miso paste 12, 16

miso curry sauce 167
sticky miso mushrooms and aubergines with creamy butter beans 176–7, **176**
mocha date shake **118**, 120, **120**
mood 12
balanced 12, 116, 184
boosters 10, 12, 16–17, 96, 150, 158, 170, 172, 180, 195, 201, 202
mousse, chocolate breakfast 36, **37**
muesli, grain-free high-protein Bircher 44, **45**
muffins
pear and walnut streusel 130, **131**
sun-dried tomato and olive 104, **105**
mushroom 39
lentil and mushroom `meatballs' with homemade tomato sauce 180–1, **180**
mushroom, bean and lentil chilli 170–1, **170**
sticky miso mushrooms and aubergines with creamy butter beans 176–7, **176**

N
Neapolitan chia pudding 116, **117**
neurotransmitters 12
noodles 16
golden miso curry noodle bowls 166–7, **166**
sesame-crusted tofu noodle salad with peanut satay sauce 84–5, **84**
nut butters 17
`nutella' (homemade) 103, 134, **135**
nutritional yeast 17
nut(s) 10, 16–17, 27, 54–5, 92
apple, date and nut breakfast oat cups 124, **125**
banana nut cinnamon rolls

122–3, **122**
caramelised nuts 36, **37**
dark chocolate Brazil nut flapjacks 186, **187**
nutty orange brain-food slaw with smoky walnuts 56, **57**
nutty pea quinoa hummus bowls 142–3, **142**
see also specific nuts

O
oat flour 133, 163, 169, 189, 190, 203
chocolate banana oat flour crêpes 134, **135**
oat(s) 12, 17, 99, 136, 181
apple, date and nut breakfast oat cups 124, **125**
brain booster creamy oats three ways **40**, 41
brain food granola 27
cherry coconut oat crumbles slices **188**, 189
dark chocolate Brazil nut flapjacks 186
matcha pistachio creamy oats 28, **29**
oils 15
olive(s) 32, 87, 156, 173
sun-dried tomato and olive muffins 104, **105**
omega-3 fatty acids 10, 30, 34, 41, 58, 79, 80, 86, 95, 104, 116, 120, 132, 146, 184, 193
orange 10
nutty orange brain-food slaw with smoky walnuts 56, **57**
orzo, beany Mediterranean orzo salad 156, **157**
ovens 19
oxidative stress 79

P
pancakes
caramelized peach and vanilla pancakes 136, **137**
red lentil pancakes with

black beans and avocado 34–5, **34**
paprika 18
`Parmesan', homemade vegan 66, 81, 151
pasta 16
beany Mediterranean orzo salad 156, **157**
green goddess pasta 80–1, **80**
one-pan courgette lasagne 164, **165**
smoky red pepper pasta salad 66, **67**
peach, caramelized peach and vanilla pancakes 136, **137**
peanut butter 27, 36, 77, 96, 100, 103, 201, 204
chocolate chip peanut butter banana bread 128–9, **128**
peanut butter and berry smoothie 118–19, 121, **121**
satay sauce 84–5, **84**, 148
Snickers-style protein bars 99
peanut(s) 12
pear and walnut streusel muffins 130, **131**
pea(s) 31, 65
nutty pea quinoa hummus bowls 142–3, **142**
pecan nut 41, 123
pepper (red) 32, 43, 53, 77, 85, 140, 144, 146, 156, 164, 171, 175, 181
red pepper pesto chickpea traybake **78**, 79
roasted red pepper 71, 87
roasted red pepper sauce 162–3, **162**
smoky red pepper pasta salad 66, **67**
peppercorns 16
pesto
red pepper pesto **78**, 79
sun-dried tomato pesto 195–7, **195**, **197**
phytochemicals 13, 148

pine nut 81, 156
pink pickles 30–1
    recipes using 48, 65, 155,
        159, 173
pistachio
    beetroot hummus with
        lentils and pistachios 152,
        153
    cacao pistachio brain
        booster creamy oats **40**,
        41
    dark chocolate avocado
        pistachio truffles 96, **97**
    matcha pistachio creamy
        oats 28, **29**
pizza, sweet potato 172–3, **172**
polyphenols 10, 13, 60, 92, 100,
    102, 116, 128, 142, 166, 201
pomegranate seed 41, 55–6,
    62, 72, 79, 155, 159, 179
potato, roasted 87
pots and pans 19
prebiotics 12, 13, 124, 128, 150,
    166, 176, 180
probiotics 12
protein 30, 34, 43, 50, 52, 58,
    62, 65, 66, 72, 76, 82, 84, 100,
    122, 144, 146, 152, 154, 156,
    172, 176, 180, 201
    the best three protein
        smoothies **118–21**, 120–1
    grain-free high-protein
        Bircher muesli 44, **45**
protein powder (vegan) 17, 28,
    44, 99, 110, 120–1, 123, 129,
    185, 203
pulses 16
pumpkin 12

Q
quinoa 16, 62, 82, 159
    nutty pea quinoa hummus
        bowls 142–3, **142**

R
radish 65, 82, 148
raisin cinnamon bagels (no-
    yeast!) 126–7, **126**
raita, cucumber 70–1, **70**, **174**,
    175

raspberry
    peanut butter and berry
        smoothie 121
    raspberry chia seed jam
        192, 193–4
    raspberry jam 184–5, **185**
    raspberry ripple layer cake
        184–5, **185**
red cabbage 85, 159
    kimchi edamame satay
        bowls 148
    nutty orange brain-food
        slaw 56
    pickled cabbage **58**, 59
rhubarb and ginger brain
    booster creamy oats **40**, 41
rice 16, 148
    coconut rice 174–5, **174**
    veggie edamame fried rice
        with sticky tofu 140, **141**

S
salads 53, 155, 173
    avocado, strawberry and
        chickpea salad 48, **49**
    beany Mediterranean orzo
        salad 156, **157**
    kale Caesar salad with
        crispy tofu 150–1, **150**
    lemony asparagus salad
        with avocado cream **64**,
        65
    Moroccan-inspired roasted
        cauliflower salad 54–5, **54**
    roasted carrot and
        chickpea kale bowls 82, **83**
    scrambled tofu hummus
        breakfast bowls 39
    sesame-crusted tofu
        noodle salad with peanut
        satay sauce 84–5, **84**
    smoky red pepper pasta
        salad 66, **67**
    sprout salad 62, **63**
    sticky tofu halloumi glow
        bowls 159
salsa
    black bean mango 178–9,
        178
    salsa verde beans 52–3, **52**

tomato **58**, 59
    tomatoes and avocado **42**,
        43
salt 16, 18
sandwich, roasted vegetable
    and salsa verde bean 52–3,
    52
satay sauce 84–5, **84**
    kimchi edamame satay
        bowls 148, **149**
sauces 82
    for creamy arrabbiata
        beans **88**, 89
    gochujang **168**, 169
    green goddess 80–1, **80**
    homemade tomato 180–1,
        180
    miso curry 167
    red pepper 66, **67**
    roasted red pepper 162–3,
        162
    satay 84–5, **84**, 148, **149**
    tahini 72, **73**
sauerkraut 12, 16, 82
seasonality 14
seed butters 17
seed(s) 10, 16–17, 27, 54–5, 65,
    104, 173
    superfood buckwheat and
        seed bread **94**, 95
    see also specific seeds
selenium 12, 142
serotonin 12, 54, 116, 120, 122,
    128, 152, 156, 158, 180, 189,
    202
sesame seed 12, 39, 72, 127,
    140, 148, 155, 167
    sesame-crusted tofu
        noodle salad with peanut
        satay sauce 84–5, **84**
shakshuka, butter bean and
    tofu feta 32, **33**
shopping list 14–18
slaw, nutty orange brain-food
    56, **57**
smoothies, protein **118–21**,
    120–1
snacks 90–110, 182–204
Snickers-style protein bars
    98–9, **98**

soup
  hidden vegetable squash
    and tomato 144, **145**
  white bean and kale 50, **51**
spelt 16, 48, 55, 65
spelt flour 17, 104–5, 130
spice mixes 71
spices 18
spinach 10, 43, 48, 74–5, 76–7,
  81, 89, 104, 121, 177
  spinach lentil fritters with
    herby yogurt 60–1, **60**
  spinach and tofu curry with
    coconut rice 174–5, **174**
  sun-dried tomato pesto
    and spinach babka 195–7,
    195, **197**
sprouted seeds/grains 146
stimulants 106, 128, 201
store cupboard staples 15
strawberry
  avocado, strawberry and
    chickpea salad 48, **49**
  Neapolitan chia pudding
    116
  peanut butter and berry
    smoothie 121
  strawberry cheesecake
    French toast 132–3, **132**
stress 12, 13, 52, 62, 140, 148,
  150, 158
streusel, pear and walnut
  streusel muffins 130, **131**
sunflower seed 12, 44, 81–2,
  196–7
  superfood buckwheat and
    seed bread 95
sustainability 14
sweet potato 36
  roasted sweet potato 71, 87
  spiced chickpea-stuffed
    sweet potatoes 72, **73**
  sweet potato falafel wraps
    with herby tahini 154–5,
    154
  sweet potato pizza 172–3,
    172
sweeteners 12

T
tacos
  black bean mango salsa
    taco bowls 178–9, **178**
  Mexican-inspired shredded
    tofu tacos 58–9, **58**
tahini 28, 53, 61, 65, 82, 203
  beetroot hummus with
    lentils and pistachios 152
  chocolate chunk tahini
    cookies 190, **191**
  herby hummus **142**, 143
  herby tahini 154–5, **154**
  homemade hummus 159
  scrambled tofu hummus
    breakfast bowls 39
  tahini dressing 87
  tahini sauce 72, **73**, 173
  tahini yogurt **42**, 43
  whipped tahini **58**, 59
tamari soy sauce 15
tart, tiramisu chocolate
  ganache 108–9, **108**
tea 10, 13
thyroid function 12
tiramisu chocolate ganache
  tart 108–9, **108**
toast
  high-protein avocado toast
    with crispy chickpeas
    30–1, **30**
  strawberry cheesecake
    French toast 132–3, **132**
tofu 12, 16
  butter bean and tofu feta
    shakshuka 32, **33**
  Caesar dressing 151
  golden miso curry noodle
    bowls 167
  green goddess pasta 81
  kale Caesar salad with
    crispy tofu 150–1, **150**
  Mexican-inspired shredded
    tofu tacos 58–9, **58**
  no nuts homemade cream
    cheese 198
  rainbow vegetable tofu
    wraps 146, **147**
  red pepper sauce 66
  roasted carrot and

  chickpea kale bowls 82
  roasted red pepper sauce
    163
  roasted squash and tofu
    sprout salad 62, **63**
  scrambled tofu hummus
    breakfast bowls 38–9, **38**
  sesame-crusted tofu
    noodle salad with peanut
    satay sauce 84–5, **84**
  spinach and tofu curry with
    coconut rice 174–5, **174**
  sticky tofu halloumi glow
    bowls 158–9
  tandoori tofu traybake with
    cucumber raita 70–1, **70**
  tofu feta 32, **33**, 48
  veggie edamame fried rice
    with sticky tofu 140, **141**
tomato 15
  beany Mediterranean orzo
    salad 156
  black bean mango salsa
    taco bowls 179
  butter bean and tofu feta
    shakshuka 32, **33**
  cauliflower gnocchi with
    red pepper sauce 163
  creamy arrabbiata beans 89
  creamy roasted butternut
    squash and spinach dahl
    77
  hidden vegetable squash
    and tomato soup 144, **145**
  homemade tomato sauce
    180–1, **180**
  mushroom, bean and lentil
    chilli 171
  red lentil pancakes with
    black beans and avocado
    34–5
  red pepper pesto chickpea
    traybake 79
  roasted aubergine and
    broccoli lentil curry 74–5
  roasted tomatoes 81, 87
  scrambled tofu hummus
    breakfast bowls 38–9, **39**
  smoky red pepper pasta
    salad 66

spinach and tofu curry with coconut rice 175
sweet potato falafel wraps with herby tahini 155
sweet potato pizza 173
tomato salsa **58**, 59
tomatoes and avocado salsa **42**, 43
white bean and kale soup 50
tomato (sun-dried) 66, 79, 146, 156, 163
sun-dried tomato and olive muffins 104, **105**
sun-dried tomato pesto 173
sun-dried tomato pesto and spinach babka 195–7, **195**, **197**
truffles, dark chocolate avocado pistachio 96, **97**
tryptophan 12, 54, 152, 180
tzatziki 168–9, **168**

U
umami 17, 140

V
vanilla 15
caramelized peach and vanilla pancakes 136, **137**
Neapolitan chia pudding 116
vegetables 14
green leafy 10, 13, 14, 38–9
roasted vegetables 71, **80**, 81–2, **83**, 87
see also specific vegetables
vitamin A 72
vitamin B6 12, 66, 122, 128, 189
vitamin B 10, 74
vitamin C 10, 74
vitamin K 10, 74

W
waffles, chickpea flour
savoury waffles with tomatoes and avocado salsa **42**, 43
walnut 10, 79, 181
apple, date and nut

breakfast oat cups 124
banana nut cinnamon rolls 123
espresso walnut cake bars 110, **111**
pear and walnut streusel muffins 130, **131**
smoky walnuts 56, **57**
wholefoods 34, 38
wholegrains 16, 41, 54–5, 82
wraps 16, 179
rainbow vegetable tofu wraps 146, **147**
sweet potato falafel wraps with herby tahini 154–5, **154**

Y
yeast 17
yogurt see coconut yogurt